*How to Be
a Friend to the Handicapped*

HOW TO BE
A FRIEND
TO THE HANDICAPPED

A HANDBOOK AND GUIDE

Leslie D. Park

VANTAGE PRESS
New York / Washington / Atlanta
Los Angeles / Chicago

FIRST EDITION

Copyright © 1987 by Leslie D. Park
Published by Vantage Press, Inc.
516 West 34th Street, New York, New York 10001

Manufactured in the United States of America
ISBN: 533-06864-9
Library of Congress Catalog Card No.: 85-91356

To the many people with handicaps
who have taught me about friendship

Contents

Preface

Sometime in our lives, almost all of us will come in contact with handicapped people. It may be an aged family member or relative who has suffered a stroke, the mentally retarded child down the street, the blind man operating the vending stand in your place of business, or the young man in your church who is in a wheelchair because of an automobile accident. Whether the contact is casual or prolonged, we all want to be helpful. The problem is that we are so unfamiliar with the situation and what is appropriate that we are often awkward, embarrassed and inadvertently cruel.

This book is intended to provide a basic guide for those who are interested in being more helpful to the handicapped people with whom they come in contact. If you have a family member with a chronic disability, quite obviously more detailed and professional counseling should be sought. Nevertheless, this is a primer for the vast majority of us who want to make our contacts with handicapped and disabled people as positive as possible.

I hope this work will serve as a reference book that will be taken off the shelf from time to time to help with specific situations. It is a distillation of many years of experience working with handicapped people and their families on a day-to-day basis. Many professional associates have had an input. Examples drawn from experience have been inserted to make certain points clear.

All in all, like a manual on a new automobile, this book will have its greatest importance when you are still new at working with a handicapped person. I hope it will become less necessary as you develop the skill and understanding needed to become the handicapped person's good friend.

CHAPTER ONE

Beginning with the Right Attitude

A friend may well be reckoned the masterpiece of nature.
— Emerson

I remember sitting in a very crowded restaurant, some years ago, during a business luncheon. Sam, an old friend from the insurance business, was my table companion. We had just ordered our meal when the headwaiter seated a middle-aged woman and her mentally retarded son next to us. Immediately, my luncheon companion became uncomforttble. When the retarded boy caught his eye, he reacted so quickly that he spilled some water on the cloth. Normal conversation was impossible and I suggested that we leave and finish our discussion in my office.

Later on, I broached the subject to Sam. He told me that he had never been comfortable in the presence of handicapped people. He said he had great difficulty with his mother-in-law, who had suffered a stroke and was now living in a nursing home. It upset him so much to visit her that he had long since given up accompanying his wife on weekend visits. This was obviously something that he felt awkward about, since he was, by nature, a rather warm and compassionate person.

What does one do in a situation like this? Sam was a success-oriented individual who put a high premium on physical appearance and well-being. He had been blessed with good health all his life, and, other than a skiing accident in which he broke his leg, he had suffered little. Sam admitted to me that he was disturbed with his attitude and wished that he felt differently. He was now in a position where he was apt to see more disability (we all do as we get older) and knew that he was making other people uncomfortable. Where could Sam begin?

Another man of my acquaintance wears a glass eye (properly called a prosthetic device). I found myself uncomfortable with him in face-to-face conversation simply because I was confused about which eye was real. The artificial eye did not focus and did not move, and it took a little time before I could get used to the fact that the good eye was really "talking" to me. Once I identified this and remembered which eye it was, I had no difficulty relating to the man in a normal manner. I became much more comfortable and now do not even consider this to be a problem.

When you come to the place where you do not remember that the person to whom you are speaking is handicapped, you probably have developed an attitude and a proper mindset that will make it possible for you and the handicapped person to become friends. It is when the handicapping condition stands between you and is an obstacle to normal relationships that you have a problem.

How can we get past this?

FEAR OF THE UNKNOWN

Almost always, the fear of the unknown determines how we respond. When a disability is thoroughly understood and "handled," either physically or psychologically, it is always easier to cope.

One of my friends with cerebral palsy tells a very amusing story of traveling on the New York City subways. She was constantly confronted by people who did not understand her spastic movements and would ask about her condition. There was never much time for an explanation, and she obviously could not go into the forms of brain injury that are responsible for cerebral palsy. Instead, she hit on a couple of phrases that she thought would satisfy most people, so that if she was leaving the subway car and was asked, "What's the matter with you?" her stock phrases were "ski jump" or "lead poisoning"!

In addition to providing some fun in an otherwise embarrassing encounter, these phrases brought some measure of the known to a condition that was (is) largely *un*known.

There is still a great deal of mystery surrounding handicapping conditions such as cerebral palsy, multiple sclerosis, stroke, muscular dystrophy, and mental retardation, to mention only a few of the common disorders. It is probably because these are largely permanent and irreversible physical maladies that the mystery persists. The causes are unknown and there are no cures.

If medical science cannot change or reverse such conditions, how can we, as ordinary citizens and friends or potential friends of the handicapped, make any difference in the life of a handicapped person? Are there things we should know and apply?

The answer is YES! *If we cannot change the physical condition, then we MUST change the environment in which the handicapped person lives. And the environment CAN BE CHANGED!*

We are a part of that environment, and we can greatly influence other parts of it. Or, to put it another way, we can bring to bear what we *know* to enhance and improve the life of the disabled person.

TREATING DISABILITY "NORMALLY"

What should be comforting to all of us as we encounter people with chronic disabilities is the fact that *virtually no chronic condition is contagious or "catching" in any way.* This, and this alone, should help us all to realize that contact with handicapped people in no way jeopardizes our own health. Armed with this bit of information, we can then go a step further in confronting the disability in the person we want to befriend.

Imagine walking into your office one morning and finding that your associate has his arm in a cast. What would be your first questions? "How did it happen?" "Where did you break it?" "How

3

long will you be in a cast?" These are natural questions raised when a person injures himself and obviously faces a convalescence. This is the cue for how we address the disabled person.

Most disabled people have those around them who "look past" their disability. They think they are being noble by ignoring the fact that the person they are talking to has an obvious physical or mental handicap. *It is a good rule that if the handicapped person we are dealing with has normal or near-normal intelligence, it is perfectly appropriate to ask him about his disability.* The very same questions are appropriate that would be addressed to the person with a broken arm. It is the normal course of friendly conversation. You will find that this clears the air immediately and makes you aware of the fact that you have an obstacle to get by in "getting to" the "person" sitting in the wheelchair. In my experience, virtually every disabled person presented with this issue has preferred to confront people with the issue of his handicap early in their association.

Where a handicapped individual is *not able* to communicate or interpret his own disability, it may be in order to inquire of family members concerning the handicapping condition. It makes *them* feel comfortable and has the same basic effect as it would have on a disabled person.

There is an important clue in this bit of behavior that is the key to all relationships that one may have with handicapped people and their families. It is the principle of normalization. *Do what you believe to be "normal" under ordinary circumstances.* The illustration of the broken arm applies here.

Not all handicapped people and their families will respond to this approach. There may be people who still disavow the fact that they have a problem and are not anxious for you to bring it up. If you sense this to be the case, then you must react differently. As a general rule, confronting the disability in a forthright manner is almost always the best way.

CALLING THINGS BY THE RIGHT NAME

There are a number of ways of dealing with a disability name that can be helpful. In my lifetime, one of the baffling medical mysteries has been the condition called amyotrophic lateral sclerosis, popularly known as Lou Gehrig's disease. It's interesting that people who contract this malady seem very anxious to identify it as Lou Gehrig's disease. He was a winner and just happened to have this particular disease. What would happen if when you were introduced to a stroke victim you said, "Oh, President Eisenhower's disease" or, in response to the person with poliomyelitis, you said, "President Roosevelt's condition"? Immediately connect the disability with a person of ability.

This is a very positive technique that needs to be practiced generally. All the poster contests and all the telethons tell us that handicapped people have abilities. Their desire to succeed more than compensates for any loss of physical function. It is wholesome, right, and humane to identify these conditions with outstanding people who have overcome similar handicaps. Do a little reading; you will be amazed at how many famous people have had chronic disabilities which are easily identified today.

I have a young friend who suffers from osteogenesis imperfecta. This was the condition commonly associated with the great electronic genius Steimetz. My friend's nickname is Steimetz, and he loves it.

The name of the physical or mental handicap may be important, but the name of the handicapped person is infinitely more important!

Try to discipline yourself to say, "John Jones is a person with cerebral palsy" rather than "He's a CP whose name is Jones." *Put the person ahead of the disability* in your conversation as much as possible. When you find that you do this naturally, you will have achieved a high level of maturity in relating to people with disabilities.

EYE CONTACT

The principle of normality should apply to other things, such as eye contact and the level and the tone of the voice. The person who normally talks to people with his head down gives away his self-consciousness when he talks to a handicapped person by looking him right in the eye! Carry on as normal!

If you find that your normal eye contact area is uncomfortable, then find some other contact area. A young lady who has a very severe winestain birthmark across half of her face often comes to my office. I found it quite difficult to have face-to-face contact with her. This was a situation she faced every day of her life. Eventually, I discovered that she had a beautiful head of hair. I taught myself to let my eyes wander to her hair during our conversation. I immediately sensed that she was comfortable with this, and I found myself more relaxed in face-to-face conversation with her. This new eye-focus area helped us both.

We usually look at a person's face during conversation. If a handicapped person has an unattractive mouth, then look at the eyes, the hair, or some other facial feature. Avoid looking at a feature that you find unpleasant, because your reaction will surely show on your face.

If looking at the face is too difficult, then find some physical attribute that you are at ease with and make that your primary point of contact. Even an article of clothing or jewelry can give you an eye "base." This takes some thinking and a little experimentation, but it is essential in order to carry on a conversation and a normal relationship.

WHAT YOUR VOICE SAYS
TO THE HANDICAPPED PERSON

There is a natural tendency for all of us to deal with handicapped people (a) as if they were children and (b) as if they could not hear or understand us. What this tends to do is to make us speak in rather childish language and generally to speak loudly when a normal tone of voice is perfectly appropriate. In research done with people who were blind, it was found that nonblind people almost always increased decibels in their voice when speaking, *yet there is really nothing wrong with the blind person's hearing!*

If we are to deal with handicapped people on the principle of normalization, then we must learn to avoid these pitfalls. Certainly, if the disabled person we are speaking to does not understand us or we do not understand him, we must change our communication style. This may mean *slower speech,* not necessarily childish phrases. If, for some reason, we cannot be heard, it may mean *speaking more clearly* rather than speaking more loudly.

A voice can also introduce an affected pity that is much resented by most disabled people. It's an element that enters the voice and yet does not really do anything to lift self-esteem or to establish a meaningful rapport between you and him. Once again, it becomes a part of the problem of "getting past the disability."

Frequent contact with disabled people will usually eliminate this problem. However, if your contacts are infrequent, it is generally a good idea to "rehearse" conversation so that you are comfortable with it.

I know a woman who has been taking care of her paralyzed husband for many ears. As a part of her regular routine, she "practices" conversation with him in front of a mirror. Oftentimes, she sees indicators that she does not want to communicate to this person she dearly loves. She is quite honest in recognizing that she has a tendency to become clipped and somewhat abrasive. Watching her own face as she rehearses her conversation with him has taught her to be more kindly and gentle in her approach—not a bad tactic.

COMMUNICATING MEANINGFULLY

Although many handicapped people, especially those who have difficult speaking, have developed their own technique and style of *leading you into appropriate conversation,* it is important to "slow down" in both listening and speaking when you are in discussion with such a person. There is a great tendency to want to finish a sentence for a disabled person and "guess" at what he is trying to say. This is generally *not* a good idea unless it is something that the person himself has asked you to do. Although it may speed up conversation, it denies the disabled person the right of his own communication, even though it may be slower and require some deciphering.

How would you treat a member of your family who contracted laryngitis for a day or two and could not communicate with you? Do the same for the handicapped person. Even though a communication problem may be permanent and irreversible, it will generally yield to some patience and a lighthearted approach.

TOO MUCH HELP MAY NOT BE HELPFUL

It is quite common to extend help to handicapped people beyond the degree required. Often a person in a wheelchair with spastic hands reaching for a pillow will find that someone leaps to his assistance, picks up the pillow, puts it behind his back (when he really wants it under his knees), and in a sense "over-helps." There is the fine distinction between useful assistance and overdoing it. Generally speaking, handicapped people should be allowed to function as independently as possible, unless they specifically ask for help or it is apparent that they are getting into difficulty because of their own limitations. *Then help should be offered.* Questions like, "Will you need any help with your coffee, Susan?" are always appropriate. Assistance when a person falls or looks like he will not be able to recover from a stumble should be spontaneous.

Offering help with "things" should be generous, and we need not give a second thought to it. Opening doors for a person in a wheelchair and removing obstacles so that a person who is blind can easily cross the room, these are just routine and common sense courtesies that need not be a problem. What *is* a problem is the assistance that may say to the person, "You're handicapped and can't do things for yourself."

Kidding and fun can often lighten helping moments. When the kidding is directed at yourself, rather than the handicapped person, you can relieve the strain from many situations.

I remember being in the presence of a very sensitive and clever person who was having coffee with a handicapped young woman. Obviously, the young lady with cerebral palsy was having trouble getting cream and sugar into her coffee and handling the porcelain cup. She was conscious of spilling coffee as she drank. It was a very clever host who directed attention to himself when he said, "Gee, I hope I can get this hot coffee past my sensitive tooth."

SPECIAL ATTITUDES
TOWARD HANDICAPPED CHILDREN

Almost all children who are mentally retarded or physically handicapped, unless their condition makes them physically fragile, should be treated the same as other children. Children love to be thrown around, to be handled, and to be active physically, and friendly roughhousing is a very positive activity. Mentally retarded children, particularly love physical contact with others. The child with Down's syndrome (in the past, incorrectly called Mongolism) is a very loving human being and will appreciate the closeness of physical contact. He is the child who will throw his arms around you instinctively. This is often embarrassing to people unless they are prepared for it.

I have found that many children love to be tickled! In playing with young spastic children, I have had some of the best times with a group of children on the living-room floor or on mats in a playroom where we tried to tickle one another to the point of hysterical laughter. There is something very intimate about this, and yet it is the stuff of normal play. (Don't try to tickle unless you are good at it!)

Good judgment dictates that we should be sensitive about the *kind* of play and the *objects* of play introduced to handicapped children. This will be dealt with more fully in later chapters; however, it would be cruel and insensitive to give a fragile toy to

9

a child with spastic hands. He may break the toy immediately and thus any possibility of your developing a relationship with him is destroyed. Simple wooden or soft material toys that are unbreakable offer the best material for playthings.

CHAPTER TWO

Begging and Buying

And a certain man lame from his mother's womb was carried, whom they laid daily at the gate of the temple which is called Beautiful, to ask alms of them that entered into the temple.

—Acts 3:2

Meeting handicapped people in the community may take many forms. We may not be very conscious of a handicapepd individual who is in his usual place each day, a person who is a part of our routine social landscape. It is quite amazing that people who take a regular route to their jobs often encounter handicapped people and do not recognize the special circumstances of these encounters.

For many months, I made a practice of purchasing my morning newspaper at a certain newsstand in New York City. This was a routine matter, and I paid no particular attention to the vendor. One summer day, I noticed that some of his newspapers had been knocked onto the sidewalk. I called this to his attention. He smiled sheepishly and said, "Would you mind picking them up? I'm crippled, you know." You can imagine my embarrassment. Even though I am a professional in the rehabilitation field, I had never noticed that this man, who always waited on me in a sitting

11

position, was a paraplegic.

It is quite obvious that we should *not* go out of our way to *find* disabilities, *notice* disabilities, or make an issue of somebody's handicap. This is contrary to all that we want to be or to do. Nevertheless, it is important to identify limitations in people who are a part of the fabric of our lives. Some situations occur repeatedly that require some special discussion.

THE HANDICAPPED STREET BEGGAR

In *Moby Dick,* the classic epic of the whaling era, Herman Melville describes a handicapped beggar:

> On Tower Hill, as you go down to the London dock, you may have seen a crippled beggar (or cadger, as the sailors say) holding a painted board before him, representing the kind of scene in which he lost his leg. There are three whales and three boats; and one of the boats (presumed to contain the missing leg in all its original integrity) is being crunched by the jaws of the foremost whale. Anytime these ten years, they tell me, has that man held up that picture and exhibited that stump to an incredulous world. But the time of his justification has now come. The three whales are as good whales as were ever published in Wapping, at any rate: and his stump as unquestionable a stump as any you will find in the western clearings but, though forever mounted on that stump, never a stump speech does the poor whaleman make; but, with downcast eyes, stands ruefully contemplating his *own amputation.*

Although it is more evident in large cities, one will generally find any populated area inhabited by one or more handicapped people who are "begging." This begging takes many forms, including the wearing of signs, tin cups, or boxes filled with relatively low-cost merchandise, such as pencils, flowers, matchbooks, et cetera. Make no mistake about the fact that all of this is begging, even though there may appear to be something for sale.

Street beggars are a phenomenon known all over the world. In many countries, begging by the handicapped is legitimized by government rules and regulations assigning appropriate space on the sidewalk or prohibiting competitive nonhandicapped people from begging. Industrialized countries, who consider themselves technically advanced, are usually embarrassed by the handicapped street beggar. *I* am embarrassed by the handicapped street beggar. It usually represents *our* failure to make the handicapped person's integration into our so-called "normal" society a reality. Nevertheless, it is not for us to develop judgments about why people are on the street begging. Our question really should be how may they be given a more effective role in society?

What do you do when a handicapped beggar is encountered on the street?

Over the years, I have developed a technique that works well *for me.*

In the first place, because of my own strong Christian ethics, I believe that it is right *for me* to give money *unconditionally* to anyone in need who asks for it. Whatever I have in my pocket should be shared.

Second, I want the person who receives my money to think of himself as a person and not an object of charity. For this reason, I ask the person his name. This tells him that I recognize him as a person. *There is nothing quite as personal as one's name!* It is true that a street beggar may give you a false name or tell you his nickname. I don't really think this matters. What is important is that you have recognized him as a *person* who has a name. You may even tell him *your* name. This is always an edifying and uplifting process. Don't pass by a person asking for help without identifying him as a human being with the same credential in the world as you have—a name!

It is quite interesting to watch the effect this has. The handicapped person will almost surely *remember you,* whether or not you remember him. If you would reach out to a needy person in such a modest personal encounter, you will do well to ask him his name.

Third, I have disciplined myself to ask each street beggar if he would mind if I prayed for him. This is obviously a very personal thing with me. It relates human need to my own responsibility.

One who is motivated by human rather than religious standards might very well ask the question, "Would you mind if I stopped by next week to see how you are doing?" or "Would you mind if I tell some of my friends that you need help?"

You see, a *continuing responsibility* is indicated by such statements. But we must mean it! Nothing is more of a fraud than insincerity. The lives of handicapped people are littered with those who have made promises and not kept them. Your promise to pray for a handicapped person or send along a friend had better be for real!

This is only one technique, and any thoughtful and sensitive person may want to develop his own technique. I have found that this works for me and makes me comfortable with the responsibility I feel toward handicapped people.

BUYING FROM HANDICAPPED SALESPEOPLE AND BUSINESSES OPERATED BY THE HANDICAPPED

Very few of us have not been approached to buy light bulbs, brooms, greeting cards, magazine subscriptions, or other goods from disabled salespeople. More and more these solicitations are made over the telephone and there is little or no way of knowing if the person is really disabled. It is difficult to know whether these solicitations are really another form of begging.

You should obviously protect yourself against any fraudulent solicitation in whatever way you can. Normally, it is important to ask for credentials, some evidence that would assure you of legitimate activity. Many people have been cheated by salespeple who represented their products as being made by the handicapped, or said that profits would go to the benefit of organizations serving the handicapped. Let the buyer beware!

14

Because the term "handicapped" or "disabled" is introduced into the sales pitch is no reason for you to be less insistent on knowing that the product and the salesperson are legitimate.

Some rules might help to guide you in this situation:

1. Never pay for products in advance. If, on the product's delivery, you find the product to be of the advertised standard and quality, then payment should be made promptly.

2. If a product is represented to you on behalf of a charitable organization or handicapped-workers cooperative, make your check (do not pay cash) to that organization or the cooperative. Never make out a check to an individual.

3. Don't buy merchandise from an organization that does not have a legitimate address and phone number. If you are sufficiently interested in the organization, call or write to inquire concerning the legitimacy of the product or the solicitation.

4. Promptly report fraudulent activity to the Better Business Bureau, the Consumers' Office in your community, or the Chamber of Commerce.

5. You have no obligation to pay for unsolicited merchandise, whether or not it represents a benefit to the handicapped.

6. Patronize handicapped workers who are in legitimate businesses. You can generally learn of such endeavors in your own community by contacting organizations and agencies serving the handicapped. Many legitimate organizations interested in the handicapped regularly have boutique sales, Christmas sales, and similar activities. Under these circumstances you can generally be sure that a very large percentage of your dollar will be used to sponsor meaningful activities for the handicapped.

7. Make a distinction between a charitable contribution and the purchase of merchandise from the handicapped. The merchandise should be worth what you are paying, while the contribution should be made without concern for any value you are receiving.

CHAPTER THREE

Appearance Makes a Difference

Clean-shaven and washed, I found that people accepted me readily.

—Disabled veteran

One of the great horrors of institutional life in the United States in recent years has been the unkempt and disheveled appearance of institutionalized people, *largely due to the type of institutional clothing provided.* The mentally retarded adolescent wearing ill-fitting, baggy trousers, dirty shoes, and a woolen shirt that is improperly buttoned is usually a "turnoff" in terms of social contact. The same person in well-fitting clothing, properly washed, and "not smelling" becomes socially acceptable immediately.

The same principles apply to handicapped people living in a private home! Many disabled people attest to the fact they are simply demeaned when their parents or assistants do not shave or wash them regularly. Most disabled people are obviously uncomfortable in the presence of others in this unkempt fashion. Good grooming is important to anyone's dignity. Almost everyone likes to be dressed nicely. This is certainly true of handicapped people.

The most seriously retarded child with any personal awareness enjoys being fussed over and cleaned up and brought into the presence of others who are "cleaned up." Behavioral scientists remind us that animals in the wilderness are never dirty. There is a level of social behavior that *must* be maintained in human beings who rely on others for their appearance.

APPROPRIATE CLOTHING

I remember directing a summer camp for handicapped young adults and teenagers. The camp was for severely handicapped people who were mostly spastic and mentally retarded. One mother brought her seventeen-year-old to the camp in very stylish "college" clothes—colored socks, a cardigan sweater, and designer jeans. It was amazing to see the ready acceptance by the *camp staff without knowing a single thing about this boy!* A wise mother had learned that this was the way young people dressed and this was the way her son would be more readily accepted.

In calling on an aged and infirm church member some years ago, I had occasion to come into his modest home and found him dressed in a stylish sweater, cleanly shaven, well-groomed, and sitting in his wheelchair. I was immediately impressed with his appearance and related to him *not* as an old and infirm man, but as a former corporate chief who was now in retirement. His appearance made all the difference in the world!

The purchase of special clothing may be a problem; however, recently there have developed a fair number of places that sell simple adapted-clothing devices: velcro fasteners instead of snaps and buttons, slip-on rather than laced shoes, oversized zippers, and support hosiery. These are all available in the marketplace and can be used by disabled people when necessary. In many instances simple innovation makes it possible to dress disabled people comfortably and stylishly.

What happens when you meet a disabled person and/or his family and find that they are always disheveled and ill-groomed? You are repulsed by his and/or their appearance. Is there any diplomatic way you can suggest that grooming is a serious problem? There are obvious and subtle ways that the subject may be broached.

One friend of mine was sensitive to this issue and made it a point to talk about grooming to parents of handicapped people. He got to the subject by saying how much he appreciated meeting handicapped people who cared for themselves properly and were dressed appropriately. The message got through.

Another technique is to fuss over new clothing a handicapped person may be wearing. Handicapped women like to be complimented on their hair or on an article of clothing or jewelry. We need to work at this harder with disabled people, since they are more sensitive about appearance. Flattery can be overdone; however, it is an important area of positive reinforcement when we can offer a meaningful compliment to someone who deserves it.

GETTING RID OF BODY ODORS

Many handicapped people have conditions that make body odors quite common. It is important to do everything humanly possible to avoid odors that would make a person socially unacceptable. No one wants to be around people who smell.

Caring for disabled people who cannot handle their own personal hygiene poses a real problem. When a person is unable to brush his teeth or clean his own mouth, it may be necessary for his personal attendant or family member to do this for him. Where a person is unable to clean himself after having relieved himself, it is essential that someone is available who can make sure that he is clean. Body odors tend to accumulate when neglected.

Any primer of concern for disabled people must begin with cleanliness and personal hygiene. Although this is discussed more fully in later chapters, it must be understood clearly that self-respect and acceptance by the world are closely tied to good grooming and personal appearance.

BEGINNING WITH THE HEAD AND THE HAIR

Since the face is really the only "naked"part of the body in normal social contact, it is the most essential part of the body to keep acceptable in appearance. One can hide scarred and deformed limbs, but cannot hide a dirty head or face.

Handicapped people should pay strict attention to the cleanliness and condition of their hair. Except in the most unusual handicapping problems, hair is generally "normal," in that it is full and has standard texture. For this reason, many handicapped people would do well to highlight their hair. A disheveled and unkempt head of hair on a person who is in a wheelchair or using crutches or a walker immediately diminishes his appearance. If the hair is unclean or the scalp is scaly and unhygienic, it is almost always an indication that other parts of the body are not clean.

Friends and relatives of handicapped men should make every effort to encourage good grooming with respect to haircuts, hairstyling, and keeping the hair combed and washed at all times. We are in an era of particularly high sensitivity to hair grooming for both men and woomen. This makes it doubly important to see that a handicapped person manages his hair and head effectively. Regular trips to a beauty salon featuring unisex hairstyles is not out of order for the disabled male.

For handicapped women, regular styling and washing of the hair is a must! Wherever possible, handicapped women should be encouraged to look after their own hair. Where this is not possible, friends and family can be very helpful.

Changing hairstyles occasionally can be a real morale booster to the handicapped woman. When well advised, hairstyle changes can bring out positive facial features and improve the appearance greatly. Dyeing of the hair is not recommended unless there are compelling reasons for doing so. "Bottle" blonds do not always have more fun! Where hair dye may be necessary to even out patchy hair discolorations or provide a better cosmetic effect, there are certainly no objections to it so long as it is kept up.

Handicapped women should learn hair care at a very early age. Wise parents will put an appropriate emphasis on this so that handicapped children do not grow up unconcerned about the style, condition, and appearance of their hair. It becomes many times more important when one is in a wheelchair! Incidentally, what is more pleasant than having a friend "do your hair"? Hair grooming offers a special and intimate opportunity for friends to participate in personal hygiene *with* disabled people.

SKIN AND COMPLEXION

Any discussion of complexion begins with soap and water. When the skin is cleaned and washed regularly, it always provides a more inviting aspect. Handicapped people should wash somewhat more frequently because of tendencies to spill and to be sloppier in eating. Washing with a mild soap and rinsing in clear water is still good advice for regular skin care.

In winter weather or under extremely drying conditions, it is probably good to apply a small amount of olive oil or some skin moisturizer on a daily basis. This can prevent dryness and scaling, which can be unusually unsightly on a disabled person.

Obtaining a light suntan during the summer months always adds to appearance. Forget about skin cancer! In discussions with numerous dermatologists, I have received the advice that the added appearance of a nice tan more than compensates for any minor risk that might otherwise be present. Good judgment should be exercised. Of course, anyone with a raw sunburn is both uncomfortable and unattractive.

Wigs

As many nonhandicapped women have found, an attractive wig can be a great personal asset. Handicapped women with thin or unattractive hair may consider regularly wearing wigs when in public. A well-kept set of wigs can be a real morale builder; however, a wig should never be put on a dirty head!

Facial Hair

Handicapped women should be especially sensitive to unsightly

20

facial hair, which may be common in many disabling conditions. Regular electrolysis or use of a depilatory cream should be a part of grooming. Parents caring for disabled adults should also be sensitive to this problem. If a person is to be at his best, then he must look his best. Facial hair never adds to appearance. Good friends and family members may be the only people to broach this sensitive subject.

Beards and Mustaches on Handicapped Men

It is very much a "macho" look for disabled men to sport a mustache or a beard. At a recent international conference, I did not see a single handicapped man in a wheelchair without a beard or a mustache! When properly groomed, cleaned, and trimmed, beards and mustaches are very attractive indeed. Although many of the wheelchair-bound "macho" types are given to wearing casual clothing and loose-fitting shirts, if their faces are clean and the beards and mustaches are properly trimmed, they retain a well-groomed and clean appearance. However, when the casual wear is accompanied by an unkempt facial appearance, they are a real "turn-off."

Friends and family members will never let disabled contemporaries think they are keeping up with current fashion by being disheveled or ungroomed!

Special Problems: Excessive Drooling and Saliva Production

In a wide variety of handicapping conditions involving the mouth, there may be a tendency to excessive drooling. Such drooling can be controlled to some degree by medication. If one has not seen a physician about this problem in the last five years, he should by all means do so. The array of pharmaceutical products to relive such conditions is impressive and growing continually. However, where drooling is an ucontrollable phenomenon, special attention should be given to bibs or other protective devices that are acceptable aesthetically and prevent the handicapped person from being wet all day long. Medical advice is required here.

CLOTHING

Special Considerations for Brace Wearers

A large number of disabled people are required to use metal braces in order to get around. Normally, these are accompanied by crutches. In some instances, braces are used with wheelchair mobility. Because of their metallic surface, braces are particularly rough on clothing, furniture, and fabrics. Some recent work in England indicates that the most satisfactory answer to those who wear "calipers" (the name for braces in England) is the "double patching" of clothing with hard-wearing materials on the interior surfaces. This makes wear and tear on the knees, elbows, and seat especially difficult. Double reinforcing can help alleviate excessive wear. This is a real budget-saver in this day and age of designer jeans!

As handicapped children grow, parents and relatives should be especially sensitive to their desire for more acceptable clothing, "like their friends." A thirteen- or fourteen-year-old boy in braces is not going to be content with oversized, baggy pants. He will want jeans just like his friends. Likewise, the handicapped young lady who approaches her adolescence will not be content with having her hair in little-girl ringlets when all her friends are wearing a more modern style. These are areas of great sensitivity that have much to do with creating a positive body image on the part of handicapped children. It is a particularly sensitive area at a time of adolescence and should get appropriate attention and be anticipated as children grow.

Footwear

Although a person may be unable to walk or move about on his own, he must still wear footwear. If an older person who is unable to move is constantly in his wheelchair in a pair of worn and dirty slippers, he looks like an old and dependent individual. If that same person puts on a pair of stylish and comfortable shoes, his appearance will improve immediately. This same principle applies to women.

Generally, footwear for the handicapped should meet some or all of the following criteria:

1. It should be comfortable *and* functional. If the function is simply cosmetic, to keep the feet covered, then the footwear should be loose and worn with stockings of the appropriate style and absorbency.

2. Where a person may do occasional walking, footwear should be secure and therapeutic. Most handicapped people would prefer footwear styles they are used to and have grown up with during their lives.

I remember one farm boy who was totally uncomfortable in his patent-leather shoes. He was much more at home and comfortable in the high-top work shoes he had seen on other family members and had worn most of his life before he had been disabled. When these were kept clean and tied, they were perfectly appropriate. Unless a disabled person is bedridden, footwear is unusually visible all day long. This alone is sufficient reason to give it some special attention.

Underclothing

Clean and laundered underclothing is a must for disabled persons. In many instances, handicapped people find that *two* changes of underclothing per day are necessary. Where soiling, excessive perspiration, or other problems are evident, there should be no question about more frequent changes.

Once again, the problem of underclothing relates to style as well as function. The handicapped person's image of himself is as important as the utility of the clothing. Unfortunately, in recent years too much attention has been given to utility. For this reason, young handicapped women do not wear the attractive lingerie and underclothing worn by others. This can often diminish one's self-image and is grossly unfair to disabled people. Wherever possible, try to balance out both utility and style so that the handicapped person is happy with his appearance and comfortable at the same time.

The Incontinent Handicapped Adult

Although it is not our purpose to enter into a full discussion of all the appropriate appliances and medical devices available to incontinent handicapped people, it may be said with some certainty that *there is simply no reason for any handicapped person to go through the day uncomfortably wet or soiled.* Modern pharmaceutical techniques and available appliances can help to keep people clean and dry for long periods.

Major considerations in controlling incontinence are (1) the comfort of the person and what is best for him and (2) social acceptability through the elimination of any odors. Under the conditions known in most countries today, these criteria can be met easily. Visits to hospital-supply stores and regular medical advice should be supplemented by perusals of catalogues that carry descriptions of the appropriate therapeutic device for controlling bowel and bladder incontinence.

Dressing for Others

Although we all tend to choose clothing that satisfies our personal taste, most of us also dress in response to the likings of those around us. The point is clear: *we dress for others as much as we dress for ourselves.*

Because of this, among handicapped people it is very important to develop some sense of dress that is appropriate to their circumstances and the friends surrounding them. The handicapped young adult who is working in a sheltered workshop doing industrial work may tend to become very sloppy in his personal appearance. If the work is particularly dirty, it only compounds the situation. The same adult working in a clerical training position will find he has to put on a dress shirt and wear a tie and perhaps even a suit jacket. His appearance will be dictated by the circumstances in which he finds himself.

In almost every instance handicapped people tend to be dressed "down" rather than dressed "up." This practice can undermine morale and discourage nonhandicapped people from developing relationships. Disabled people have enough difficulty seeing themselves as people of worth without the added burden of sloppy dress habits.

Do what you can to encourage appropriate and stylish dressing!

When the trend is toward casual dress, encourage more formal dress as a change.

If the handicapped person's dress is inappropriate, by all means say something to him. Say it kindly, say it helpfully, but say it!

CHAPTER FOUR

Gifts for the Handicapped

The gift tells what you think of the person.
—Advertisement

At one time or another, you might find it appropriate to provide gifts for a handicapped child or adult, aged relative or friend, or a person who is chronically infirm. I am not talking about the type of gift that one might give to a friend who is in the hospital for a week. That is another category and I would not consider such a person handicapped unless he had a chronic condition.

Gifts and special remembrances speak very clearly about how we regard the handicapped. Believe it or not, gifts can be cruel! Though never intended, they provide telltale signs of how we regard a person.

GIFTS OF ADVENTURE

Probably nothing provides as much permanent value to a disabled person as a gift that in some way attaches him more securely to the world at large. For example: I remember when a good friend of mine provided a special birthday gift to a handicapped young woman in a wheelchair that included two tickets to the ballet, taxicab vouchers, and a reservation at a nearby restaurant. With the tickets went specific intructions concerning what theater entrance to use (one entrance was barrier-free) and information on how to get to the restaurant easily. You probably guessed that this was the highlight of that person's year and no gift would have been more meaningful.

Such a gift provided an opportunity for this disabled person to do something she would never do normally, something her family would never consider. As it turned out, this young woman decided to treat her mother to the ballet and the two of them had one of the most enjoyable evenings of their lives.

Another instance I recall occurred when some friends of a disabled man arranged for him to have dinner at a very special restaurant and notified the restaurant of this man's disability and the fact that it was a special event. The restaurant staff went out of their way to make this a memorable occasion for all concerned.

Quite obviously, these are special gifts for special friends, but they indicate imagination and style, which greatly helps the handicapped person.

Two elderly friends who are very dear to me spent a very special day visiting one of the new buildings in New York City as an anniversary gift. The giver carefully chose the time of day when the two elderly people would meet the smallest crowds and have the least problem with transportation. It was a really memorable outing, clever and unusual.

GIFTS TO AVOID

In my conversations with disabled people, many have revealed that they like to receive gifts that are not aimed at being "special for the handicapped." One young lady I know spoke somewhat sheepishly about her handicap, which makes it impossible for her to fasten her brassiere from the back. Apparently, every relative was aware of the situation, and she said, "Do you realize how many bras I have that fasten in the front?" It turned out that these bras had been given to her by every relative she had.

Generally speaking, gifts are *special* and should stand out from the ordinary. If a handicapped person in your acquaintance does not have a warm shirt, then the most appropriate gift may be a warm shirt. (Let's hope it's stylish and was selected tastefully.) The older person who spends much of his time at home and may be infirm is generally a recipient of several dozen warm shirts from family and friends each year. The blind person usually has a half-dozen radios, and the partially bedridden person can show you a drawer full of bathrobes in various styles, colors, and sizes!

Think twice before you buy what appears to be practical. Use a little imagination in selecting gifts. Go for style. The handicapped person generally appreciates this very much. Whatever you do, bring some class into whatever you select.

In many ways, gifts should be no different than those you would select for your nonhandicapped friends; however, you do have to be somewhat discriminating. It is generally a good idea *not* to be "therapeutic" with the gifts you select. Many disabled people have been advised by doctors and other medical people all their lives and their families have become real experts at knowing what they need.

If your acquaintance with a handicapped person is casual, don't become a sudden therapy expert by selecting a nonslip drinking glass with a rubber bottom because you think it would be helpful. Talk to the family first. You might even casually discuss the need for this type of utensil with the disabled person himself. If he responds positively, it may be a cue; nevertheless, you are much safer staying away from gifts that are in any way related to the handicap. There are obvious exceptions to this rule, and if something "jumps out at you," by all means consider it.

Recently, I saw a "whistle switch" device advertised in a newspaper. I sent for it and found it to be an extremely useful little plastic squeezer with a receptacle box that fits into an electrical outlet, making it possible to turn on lights and any electrical switches by simply squeezing the device. It emitted a high-pitched whistle, thereby energizing the electricity. A person in a wheelchair, by simply squeezing the whistle, is able to turn off lights, radio, et cetera. I bought the device and gave it to a handicapped person as a "gimmick gift." I really did not know whether it was appreciated or whether it would work. To my pleasant surprise, it was a real hit and the young lady who received it sent for several more and now has them throughout her apartment. Truly, this gift made her life much simpler. Although related to the handicapping condition, it was unusual, imaginative, and unlikely to be selected by others.

If you are in doubt about gifts, why not make a list of options and present them to the handicapped person himself? How about a list for a teenage person in a wheelchair that might go like this:

Happy birthday, George. I was in so much doubt about what you would most enjoy that I am offering you a choice:

1. tickets to the Jets game (if you don't have a friend that would like to go along with you, I'll be glad to do the driving and be your "pusher" for the evening);
2. that Christian Dior shirt you admired in the magazine;
3. since you're such a baseball nut, an autographed copy of *The Bronx Zoo*;
4. dinner and movie at places of your own choice.

SPECIAL GIFTS FOR HANDICAPPED CHILDREN

Toys are truly the tools of children. They represent the hardware of learning at an early age. If you are considering toys as gifts, it becomes very important that you give special attention to certain aspects of the toy world; this will be appreciated by young handicapped children.

Since the range of handicapping conditions is so complex, it is difficult to be specific when discussing appropriate toys. Generally speaking, toys should be selected because they are fun to handle. Handicapped children very often appreciate sensory stimulation from the toys they play with. The cuddly stuffed toy may be especially meaningful to a handicapped child because he loves to feel the texture of the fur on his face. Or a sturdy, well-finished wooden toy may provide just the right invitation to an unsteady grasp.

Easily broken toys are never appropriate.

Be very careful of toxic and flammable materials.

Remember that in the hands of a disabled child, the problems of children's toys are compounded many times over. A sharp edge on a toy that would be handled carefully by a child who is not handicapped becomes dangerous to the child with spastic hands, or the blind child.

Consider making and adapting toys. Many electronic and battery operated toys can be adapted easily to meet the needs of children who have handicapping conditions. There are a large number of switching mechanisms available that enable the child who can only use a foot or a knee to turn on a switch. Some toys may be energized by simple pneumatic pressure produced by sucking and puffing. For some quadriplegic children, these toys are easily controlled.

There is at least one child in my acquaintance whose father, with no special knowledge of electronics, developed a train set that can be controlled completely by his handicapped son who uses a suck-and-puff switching mechanism. What a thrill it is to see this boy in his wheelchair, wearing his engineer's hat, controlling the trains with a simple cigar holder attached to a plastic tube!

Persons who have sewing skills will often find that a disabled person has great appreciation for any handmade item. A shirt with monogrammed initials or a dress that is made to the stylish measurements of a young woman in a wheelchair is really something special. If you have special hobbies of your own, you may consider getting a handicapped person involved in your hobbies by giving him a "starter kit."

Many handicapped people are very observant and make good collectors. If you are into collecting stamps, coins, matchbooks, or bottle caps, why not consider a gift that would start your disabled friends on a similar collection? Just think of all you will have to talk about as you get to know each other better!

As you learn of the special interests and abilities of a handicapped child, you will soon find yourself shopping in toy stores, book shops, and department stores with a new kind of orientation. That's great! I am sure it will pay off in the imaginative things you bring into that disabled child's life.

Don't forget that special gifts of services may be both unusual and useful for the handicapped recipient. Do you remember how special you felt after that unusual hairstyling trip to the beauty shop? How about a special manicure or a facial?

Books and subscriptions to magazines are always good gifts. Incidentally, why not consider the purchase of a special electric page-turner for those who may not have this facility themselves? Such devices are available through catalogue sales of equipment for handicapped people. A page-turner is unusual enough to be considered special and not "handicapped stuff."

Gifts of flowers, dish gardens, or bonsai plants may also be something very special in the lives of disabled people.

The gift of a party may be a real treat. The friend or family member who shows up with half a dozen good friends in party hats for a special occasion is always a welcome sight! Be creative and, by all means, be sensitive. A party, when a family member is in the hospital, might be cruel.

Handcrafted and personalized hobby items make unusual and special gifts. One of the prize possessions in the otherwise bleak existence of a handicapped young woman is a hand-stitched and embroidered framed piece on the wall that reads: "Happiness is having a home of your own, like Alice has." Obviously, Alice treasures this very much.

A friend of mine who is handy in woodworking made a special nautical sign that reads: "Hubert's Sloop." Hubert feels like he is on the bridge of his own ship when he takes his place in his wheelchair under this piece.

The thought and time that go into a gift signal the feelings of the giver. Here is your chance to reach out in warmth and friendship beyond anything you can say in words.

CHAPTER FIVE

Getting Familiar with the Wheelchair

The wheelchair is the object and symbol around which we are now designing our environment.

—An American architect

The international symbol of access for handicapped people is a graphic design of a person in a wheelchair. All over the world, the wheelchair has become symbolic of what it means to be handicapped. This is reason enough to become familiar with the wheelchair and simple techniques for helping its occupant. There is no mystery to it, and the principles are quite simple.

The best information we have indicates that wheelchairs have been around for hundreds, perhaps even thousands, of years. When a person cannot walk or move by himself, a very obvious principle is, by sitting in a large wheeled vehicle, a person can be moved more easily than being lifted or carried. This is the basic reason for wheelchairs and offers the fundamental reason why people are confined to wheelchairs.

Today there are a variety of wheelchair makers, wheelchair styles, and wheelchair sizes. You must understand this, because a wheelchair is a very personalized piece of equipment that should "fit" the handicapped person who will use it. Most manufacturers offer a variety of special features and styles. If you are in any way involved in the selection of a wheelchair, it is important to have the proper medical input as to what type of wheelchair will best serve that special disabled person. In many instances, a handicapped person will spend a very large number of his waking hours in a wheelchair. If it is not comfortable and does not fit him properly, secondary problems affecting his spine, circulatory system, and important body functions may result.

A young man I know had been sitting in the same wheelchair for many years. In the course of time, his physical characteristics changed. The wheelchair had originally been ordered for him when he was quite obese, but recently he had lost weight. He thought he was suffering some progressive deterioration, because every time he got in his wheelchair he would lose the feeling in his legs within an hour. When a careful analyis was made, it was discovered that the wheelchair was improperly fitted and the circulation in his legs was cut off when he sat in it! It is useful to be aware of possible problems since many friends have discovered difficulties that have gone undetected by the handicapped person or his family simply because they are so used to seeing a handicapped person in this familiar equipment.

If it appears that the chair is the wrong size or functioning poorly, why not ask your handicapped friend or his family about the situation? Inquire as to how long it has been since the chair was fitted and suggest that maybe some modest change would make the person more comfortable. Once again, the principle of normality is a good rule of thumb. You would not invite a person into your living room for an evening's conversation and allow him to sit in a seat that is uncomfortable.

Many wheelchair-bound persons attest to the fact that they find it useful to have more than one wheelchair. A very lightweight model may be useful for traveling, whereas a more substantial model provides the comfort needed over long hours of occupancy. Getting out of the chair periodically is a good thing to do to avoid problems of pressure and circulation.

ADAPTING WHEELCHAIRS

Comfort is obviously a primary consideration. Oftentimes, the insertion of a cushion in the seat or at the back of the wheelchair may provide an appropriate change of posture in the course of the day. If such a cushion is colorful and attractive, it becomes an important aesthetic change as well.

Teenagers particularly enjoy variety if they are in wheelchairs. One teenage paraplegic I know has a variety of different wheelchair cushions she selects according to her mood each day. Some have loud, psychedelic patterns, and others are more subdued with traditional designs. She considers this cushion selection much the same as choosing the clothing she will wear. After all, the wheelchair is a part of her physical being for most of her waking hours. As she says, "Why not jazz it up?"

Many teenagers and younger people in wheelchairs have chosen to carry slogans and symbols on their chairs, much like the current fad of bumper stickers. These can represent a kind of subtle humor that adds a very pleasant dimension to the lives of disabled persons.

CLEANING WHEELCHAIRS

Why not become a really special assistant to your disabled friend in the wheelchair by offering to clean the device? Few people think of this, yet it is a very welcome offer. All you need to clean the chair is some chrome polish (you might have some that you use on your automobile), some soap and water to clean the leather or vinyl, and perhaps, a stiff brush to get at hard-to-reach places around the spokes. Because of the very personal nature of a wheelchair, this type of cleaning is a regular requirement. Unfortunately, few handicapped people are as conscious of this "hardware hygiene" as they should be. It is not unusual to see a person in a wheelchair with the hardened remains of some food in evidence. This need not be and you can help by offering to do the cleaning.

If, while you are at it, you want to lubricate the bearings with a little light oil, it's amazing how this will help.

SIMPLE WHEELCHAIR MAINTENANCE

Unfortunately, hospitals, medical-supply stores, and other service centers require long periods of time to do the simplest of repairs on wheelchairs. Where the repairs *are* simple, you might offer to assist. Tightening bolts, tightening the spokes, or repairing the vinyl fabric on a seat is not difficult for any person who is at all handy. If the handicapped individual takes his wheelchair for repair, it often involves the chair being out of action for several weeks. It may also involve the rental of an additional chair or some other makeshift arrangement. You can be helpful in these situations by doing the job yourself if it is something you can handle.

Steam-cleaning equipment will really do a great job on a wheelchair. The steam cuts through food particles, oil, and grease and provides a thorough cleaning.

SIMPLE WHEELCHAIR AIDS

Wheelchair Trays

A simple tray that slips onto the arms of a wheelchair and provides a flat and clean surface on which to write, eat, or work is an extremely useful addition. Such a tray is constructed quite easily and involves only the simplest of measurements. A wheelchair equipped with such a tray provides a wonderful work surface for handicapped people. Books, pictures, hobby tools, and eating utensils have an immediate and appropriate surface on which to be placed. When such a tray is covered with formica, it presents a

35

clean and easily maintained surface that is immediately in front of the person at all times. Physical therapists and doctors often comment on the fact that such a surface also provides a good area for the handicapped person to rest his arms. It may improve posture greatly. Certainly, it is a desirable supplement to the wheelchair itself.

Wheelchair Carriers

A simple canvas bag or bicycle saddle carrier provides useful space for a person in a wheelchair who might have occasion to carry books, articles of clothing or small packages. Since these carriers do not come with wheelchairs and are quite costly when purchased from supply houses, they represent ideal gifts. Home-workshop construction projects can produce these carriers to assist the handicapped person. Once again, some aesthetic value should be put into such equipment. An unpainted wooden box attached to the side of a wheelchair is hardly attractive. When that box is covered with vinyl or cleverly and artfully painted, it takes on an entirely different character.

Other Useful Attachments

A rear-view mirror available at a bicycle shop may provide a very useful attachment on a wheelchair used by someone who has occasion to travel city sidewalks. Since it is virtually impossible for a person in a wheelchair to see behind him, this device offers the same type of safety factor as a mirror does to a driver in an automobile.

A very considerate wheelchair user may find that having a clean cloth in his carrier bag to wipe off the wheels before entering the carpeted floor of a home is appreciated by his parents or his hosts. It has the same effect as wiping one's shoes before going into a home. A wheelchair user's courtesy also involves avoiding unnecessary "bumping" of furniture, walls, or other parts of a home that can be damaged by this type of contact. Where the contact may be frequent and unavoidable, simple rubber bumpers can be taped or fixed to the chair to avoid any damage.

BECOMING A RELIABLE WHEELCHAIR PUSHER

Many of us are required to push someone in a wheelchair from time to time. We generally do this willingly and usually feel good about providing help of this kind. Here are some primary rules that will make the handicapped person feel more secure when you are doing the pushing:

A general rule to follow is to mount any curb or steps with the rear wheel (the large wheel) first. In most instances, this involves turning the chair around to come up backward. Usually, pulling a person up a curb or set of steps this way involves tilting the chair back slightly so that it is more or less balanced. You should then take the person up or down one step at a time. *You must be in complete control of the chair at all times.*

Always avoid tipping the chair forward, since this is hazardous to the disabled person. Many a well-meaning pusher has endangered the safety of a disabled person by tipping the chair forward and having that person spill onto the floor.

If you are pushing a wheelchair up an incline or a ramp, keep up a steady pace and avoid stopping in the middle. Develop a comfortable momentum and keep pushing until you are on a level surface. If you are entering an elevator, always turn the chair around and back into an elevator so that you can come out facing forward.

Carrying on a conversation while you are pushing a wheelchair is very difficult. It is difficult for the person in the chair to hear you, and it is almost impossible for him to communicate with you in this position. This is roughly analogous to carrying on a conversation with a person who is walking ahead of you. It is never appropriate to engage in serious conversation in this position.

IN AND OUT OF A VEHICLE

A large majority of the wheelchairs used by handicapped people are of a folding type, so that by simply pulling up on the seat or disengaging a lever the frame is no longer rigid and you can fold the chair for easy maneuvering into a car. Many taxicabs will take people in wheelchairs and assist in folding the chair. Normally, the best procedure for entering a car from a wheelchair is to bring the chair alongside the car-seat surface as close as you can get it. If the person in the chair has some use of his hands, you might roll the window down and open the car door into a fixed position. This offers some opportunity for the handicapped person to hold onto the door frame while he is assisted onto a seat. If the chair is then folded and put into the backseat or the trunk of a car, you are ready for embarkation when you stop.

It is *not* recommended that a person be transported while sitting in his wheelchair unless he is in a special vehicle that has been equipped for this purpose. Most wheelchairs are not made to withstand external forces with the body weight of the person in the chair. If a person is seated in an open van without his wheelchair attached properly to the frame of the van, he is in a very precarious position and a sure candidate for serious injury if an accident occurs. Simply propping things behind the wheels will not stop the chair from moving in a sudden stop or sharp turn. Don't try it!

SOME TIPS ON LEARNING
TO HANDLE A WHEELCHAIR

If you will be called on to handle a disabled person in a wheelchair regularly, you might want to learn how to handle it by taking an *empty* chair through its paces. While the chair is empty, maneuver it up and down stairs, through doors, into a car, et cetera. This will make you much more comfortable when you have a passenger. Another useful exercise is to actually get into the chair yourself and wheel it about to get some feel of how it handles. This helps you see how the world is perceived by the handicapped person.

A number of voluntary agencies and veterans groups have wheelchair obstacle courses so that nonhandicapped persons may have an opportunity to experience the world from the wheelchair. If you can participate in such a course, I am sure you will find it very helpful.

Almost all wheelchairs are well made and will stand up with proper maintenance and normal use.

Where wheelchairs are apt to be on the sidewalk after dark, it is a good idea to have at least one strip of reflector tape (or several bicycle reflectors) applied to both the front and back of the chair.

ELECTRIC WHEELCHAIRS

Increasingly, handicapped people who are going to be in wheelchairs for long periods of their lives are turning to electric and self-propelled wheelchairs and similar devices. Since most of these operate by battery, special care should be taken to see that battery acid is not spilled on floors when the chair is tipped. Additionally, chairs with batteries should be set up so that they can be recharged at periodic times with the least amount of inconvenience. An outlet for a battery charger should be easily accessible to the person who is required to do this as a part of his regular routine.

Persons who are facing long periods in their lives when they may be confined to a wheelchair should seriously consider the value and the cost-effectiveness of self-propelled wheelchairs. The requirements for someone to be on hand as a pusher are enormous. Wheelchairs with a simple joystick control can give new independence to many people who are otherwise totally dependent.

WHEELCHAIR SAFETY

Since all wheelchairs are equipped with brakes, it is extremely important to see that the brakes are locked when a person is getting in or out of his chair or transferring from one seat to another. If the person cannot control the wheelchair himself, you should be very sure that the brakes are locked. Be especially careful if the chair is on an incline. More than one wheelchair-bound person has been seriously injured because a careless but well meaning friend left him parked on an incline unattended. When a wheelchair gets rolling under these circumstances, it almost always involves injury to the disabled person.

If a handicapped person is to be left unattended in his chair for any period of time, be very sure that the chair is in a safe position. Locating the chair where somebody may very well round the corner and crash into it can cause a very serious situation. All these problems are compounded when the chair is left unattended out-of-doors.

Leaving the chair in a driveway or parking lot where vehicles may appear should never be tolerated. The unattended person in a wheelchair is absolutely defenseless against moving people or vehicles. On the sidewalk, this may mean bicycles and children in moving wagons or on scooters. Don't compromise the safety of a disabled person by allowing him to be the unwitting victim of a careless cyclist or child.

CHAPTER SIX

Pets, Other Animals, and the Handicapped

Whatever goes upon four legs, or has wings, is a friend.

—George Orwell,
Animal Farm

Because of their handicapping condition, disabled people are often denied normal experiences that tend to enrich life. Parents do not often consider pets for disabled children, yet there is much to be said for bringing living creatures into the lives of the handicapped.

Animals often respond to disabled people in an unusual way. The responsibility developed in taking care of an animal also adds a dimension to the life of a handicapped person, particularly a child. It generally has a salutary effect on his personality.

Most mature parents know that the cute little puppy and the cuddly little kitten will soon grow up to become an animal with a considerable life span. Responsibility for him belongs to someone. That someone is usually the parents of the child. This is normal. When families with children undertake to bring a pet into their house, they are really accepting a lot of daily responsibility. This decision should also be considered with a disabled family member. The compensating factors in pet ownership are more than worth the effort that goes into it.

In recent years, pets have become more than objects of love and care. We are all acquainted with the Seeing Eye dog and the value

41

of this type of animal to a blind person. New roles being developed for animals hold great promise for the future. Recently, dog training has been undertaken to provide animals that would do a lot of the "fetching" necessary when one is not able to get out of a chair or out of bed. Quite obviously, a dog cannot be trained to bring you a glass of water, but he certainly can bring such things as slippers, other articles of clothing, the newspaper and other objects that are a part of daily life. Training programs for these animals are now underway in several parts of the United States.

Animals also provide a great measure of security. Dogs are particularly known for their security value, and a handicapped person who may have to spend a part of his day alone usually feels very secure with an animal in the house who has been trained to guard the premises.

SELECTING A PET

Good judgment and careful thought should be entailed in the selection of a pet for a handicapped person. The handicapped individual should make the primary decision in this matter; nevertheless, his parents or friends may often temper his judgment so that a pet becomes an asset, rather than a burden and a bother.

A blind person is usually well served by pets that can be heard and/or felt. One blind person I know has several canaries. He is able to care for these birds very effectively, since virtually all of the cage-cleaning responsibilities can be carried on without sight. Of course, the constant symphony of bird song in his home enhances the quality of his life as he is able to tell which of his birds is singing and knows the special characteristics of each one. The care of birds is relatively inexpensive, and a simple call to the pet shop is usually all the advice that is needed in care and training.

Cats also make excellent pets. They are very cuddly and no one who has ever stroked a cat in an easy chair in front of a fireplace thinks there is anything quite like this experience. Cleaning and feeding a cat may require much more physical ability and effort than caring for birds. Pet experts tell us that it is usually better to have two cats than one, since the cats themselves seem to enjoy the presence of each other. It is obvious that having a cat neutered when it is to live indoors is essential.

Fish and aquarium life can be enjoyed by a large number of handicapped people. The cleaning and maintenance chores of an aquarium may require the help of an able-bodied person on a regular basis. A family member or dependable friends can often meet this need. Some who are fish hobbyists may find it especially enjoyable.

Although the relationship between a handicapped person and fish in an aquarium is vastly different than a handicapped person would have with an animal that can be heard, touched, and trained, many wheelchair-bound and bedridden people have attested to the fact that an aquarium is a constant source of visual pleasure. In a recent trip to a pet shop, I saw a father with a young mentally retarded boy selecting a new batch of tropical fish. In a brief conversation, the father said that his son had reacted to these fish as he had to no other living things. He was constantly amazed at their antics and enjoyed watching them whenever he was not otherwise engaged. The father felt that the fish brought an element to the young boy's life that had heretofore never been discovered.

Older people who are infirm seem to especially enjoy fish. The cleaning chore for the mildly infirm person is a useful regular activity that many older people actually enjoy. It is something to do, something to look forward to, and the fish are living things to care for, observe, and protect. These are necessary elements of life and relate us to the living world.

Matching the Handicapped Person with a Pet

Quite obviously the child with spastic hands who has uncontrolled movements should not handle delicate animals, or other fragile creatures. That same child might enjoy the physical contact with a large dog who would not be put off by a rough touch from a spastic hand.

Many handicapped young women who are physically incapacitated seem to enjoy cats. They offer an outlet for the mothering instinct in petting and "nonsense chatter," which is so much a part of caring for a cat.

Although hamsters, mice, and guinea pigs are often chosen by children as pets, their selection for handicapped children is not recommended unless the child is especially drawn to such animals. These are generally very fragile pets who require a lot of care and often are not the type of pets that one can keep in a living room. (Disabled people rarely go to the basement!) Good judgment should dictate whether they are appropriate for handicapped people with whom you may have contact. (Showing up with a pair of hamsters on Christmas Eve may end your friendship with that handicapped child and his family forever!)

The more exotic pets that require constant monitoring of food, temperature, humidity, et cetera, need not be ruled out when considering pet possibilities. A homebound person may prove to be a wonderful caretaker and find his life enriched when he knows he is responsible for the care of another living creature. There are those who attest to the fact that keeping reptiles and amphibian-type pets, which require careful environmental monitoring, can be done best by people who are constantly on the scene. A bedridden person who has good judgment and some functional use of his hands may very well find this to be a rewarding diversion.

ANIMALS IN THE WILD

Who of us doesn't enjoy listening to the songbirds and watching their antics in the shrubbery? Who hasn't seen squirrels and rabbits frolicking on a lawn and smiled to himself?

Two elderly friends of mine have undertaken to care for a squadron of squirrels who inhabit the woods behind their home. Much of their life is devoted to the observation, feeding, and protection of these beloved woodland friends. They appear on the back stoop regularly, climb up the screen door and occasionally enter the house to get their daily allocation of peanuts. They are called by name, and they respond! A daily ritual is established in putting out food, water, and other amenities for these furry friends. In a recent snowstorm, I remember the couple expressing their concern about the absence of the squirrels. What activity could bring more joy to the life of a handicapped person?

It takes very little imagination to develop a simple system that makes it possible for the handicapped or retarded person living at home to enjoy these pleasures. Even the most cloistered urban circumstances may permit us to bring animals and birds into our lives. One very clever British bioengineer has invented a bird-feeder that hangs on the window by a suction cup and provides a very effective and attractive feeding device for city birds. Having the birds feed right in front of the window is a unique experience.

Waking a handicapped person up in the middle of the night to watch raccoons raiding garbage cans can be fun. Don't neglect this type of experience! Handicapped people desperately need contact with the living world, and many of them find great solace in any visual or personal contact with animals. This is a pleasure often denied disabled people because they obviously cannot hike the trails of the Adirondacks or participate in the annual bird count in the wetlands. They should nevertheless be offered every opportunity to come in contact with the life of animals in the wild whenever possible.

Clever friends and family will make a real game of this. Keep your written scoreboard of when and where the rabbits are seen in each season, identify various types of birds, and record the type of food fed to the birds as the seasons change and the special characteristics of their natural life (when they feed, mate, migrate, et cetera). One New York resident even records the frequency of his encounters with the apartment cockroaches and their size (not recommended)!

THE FARM AND THE ZOO

The zoological gardens in many cities now offer special parks that allow children to pet and handle animals. This is certainly an experience that should not be denied handicapped children. It is also an experience that can be enjoyed by disabled adults and infirm aged people. A trip to the zoo is one of the best outings a family with a disabled member can enjoy.

The farm also offers a good resource for experience with animals and other natural resources. One of the most interesting handicapped people I have ever known is a young man who helps to manage a large midwestern farm owned by his father. Although the young man is wheelchair-bound, he has become a superb manager. He regularly researches farm methodology, reads all the journals, and keeps the books on the family business. This is such a big part of farming today that his handicap is no problem to successfully running this family business. Operating from his office, which is equipped with a two-way radio, he can instruct field hands on the tractors, in the barn, and others actually handling farm work. He hunts from his wheelchair in a duckblind especially constructed for him.

Strangely enough, one of his pastimes is horseback riding. Although he cannot mount or dismount by himself, he has found riding to be a most enjoyable activity and has his own horse, which is stabled with the other farm animals. Horseback riding has grown in popularity for the handicapped throughout the world. Spastic children in England are regularly provided with the opportunity of handling and riding horses. This trend has grown in the United States and there are now a fair number of clubs organized for handicapped riders found throughout the country.

A visit to a farm by a handicapped child should be a must. Some appreciation of farm animals and farm life is an important part of learning as we grow. There are those who advocate a vacation period on a farm as well. Some of the happiest days I remember as a child were spent vacationing on a farm in Michigan. There were dimensions to this life that were new to me. I remember the concern of the farmer when the deer were eating the celery plants. I never think of celery without remembering this experience.

Seeing the milking process or learning to understand how silage is made and how grain is processed is a wonderful experience for any person. It is often denied to handicapped children because we somehow remove them from any contact with this part of our world.

Parents and friends of disabled people should certainly have these opportunities in their "bag of tricks."

FISHING AND CRABBING

Living near the water offers an unusual opportunity for handicapped and infirm people to participate in a sport that brings them in touch with living creatures: Fishing is a very popular sport among disabled people. There are obvious reasons for this, yet I believe that many people who would like to befriend the disabled do not consider using this activity as part of their "contact repertoire." One of the most memorable photographs I can remember is of our paraplegic president, Franklin D. Roosevelt, sitting on the back end of his yacht with a fishing pole. A broad smile on his face indicated that he had landed a big one.

From very active fly casting and surf fishing to sitting at the end of the pier with a pole, fishing can be adapted for handicapped people in many ways. Some years ago, the very clever staff of the University of Southern Illinois developed a special fishing raft so that handicapped summer campers could fish from this canopied monstrosity safely in the middle of the lake. The raft was equipped with a simple railing and a canvas canopy and was towed by a power boat where a group of four or five handicapped peeople could dunk their poles all day long. There were some pretty good catches!

I remember taking a vacation with my young family to the Jersey shore, where we intended to enjoy a week of complete disassociation from rehabilitation work, as I had worked professionally with handicapped people all my life. Lo and behold, we found that the person in the cabin next to us was a young handicapped man with his father and mother! The father was an avid

47

fisherman and would take his son out in the boat bright and early each morning, with the catch brought home late in the morning, then cleaned and eaten for supper. I don't think I have ever seen any brighter eyes or a more enthusiastic sportsman than this young man, although he was totally handicapped and required complete physical handling by his parents. His vacation consisted of fishing with his father, and he enjoyed it with obvious relish.

CHAPTER SEVEN

Safety Standards for the Handicapped and Those Who Care for Them

A disregard for simple safety will continue to be the most serious threat to health.

—National Safety Council

Because most handicapped people are either totally or partially dependent on others, they are susceptible to the problems of accidents and calamity more than usual. For this reason, some very obvious safety practices should be instituted. Just as one is more conscious of hazardous conditions with small children, one must be extremely cautious with disabled people who can easily find themselves in situations that are potentially dangerous.

FIRE SAFETY IN THE HOME

If you have an invalid or semi-invalid person living in your home, or if you are a disabled person living alone, by all means notify your local fire department of this fact immediately. As a general rule, fire departments will identify your home with some appropriate window sticker or other record to assist them in the event of an emergency. Additionally, most local fire departments will make a visit to the home and provide practical instruction for the most suitable fire-safety precautions.

Firemen all over the United States are great friends of the handicapped. A young handicapped person in Pennsylvania lived in a modest house next to the local fire station. His entire life was enhanced by the friendship and fun he had with the firemen. He was the guest of honor at most of their fund-raising functions and was often taken on trips and excursions by members of the department.

Some simple precautions in the home can often avoid very serious potential fire hazards. Here are some simple rules:

1. If the handicapped person is immobile, try to provide sleeping quarters on the ground level of the home, preferably near an accessible exit.

2. Never permit smoking in bed by a disabled person (or any other person living in the same house).

3. Check and double-check all electrical appliances used by a handicapped person. Electric blankets, heating pads, and other sickroom electric devices should be checked periodically for safe wiring and plugs.

4. If the handicapped person is a smoker, have him use a flameless cigarette lighter.

5. Insist on flame-retardant bedclothes.

6. Buy a cooking range and oven with removable control knobs if a senile or mentally retarded person lives with you and has access to these areas.

7. Use safety covers for all electrical outlets with mentally retarded chidren or adults in the home.

8. When cooking out-of-doors, keep handicapped people well away from the fire area. Anticipate wind shifts and changes that might blow sparks in their direction.

9. Keep mentally retarded children under very close supervision during cookouts, camp fires, or fireplace activities.

Common sense rules always prevail in these matters, but there are also living areas that are especially dangerous.

BATHROOM AND HOT-WATER PROBLEMS

A young girl with cerebral palsy, who was living on her own after many years of dependency, was scalded to death in her bathtub because she slipped and could not turn off the hot-water controls. This type of tragedy is avoidable and needless. Hot-water controls that are used by the handicapped, or persons with limited judgment, should be set so that the temperature of the water is well below anything that would cause scalding (below 125° Fahrenheit).

Scalding accidents are very common among handicapped people. If possible, serious consideration should be given to providing shower controls *outside* of the shower stall or tub. This provides for a control of the water temperature *before* an individual is actually under the stream. Able-bodied persons, including family members, are then able to set the temperature controls for the disabled person so that he is not dependent upon his own abilities to do this.

New devices now on the market make it possible for a pre-set temperature to be energized by simply putting one's hands under the spigot. An electric "eye" turns the water on and off without the need for twisting handles. Devices of this kind are well worth the investment in terms of peace of mind and the actual reduction of safety hazards.

HAZARDOUS UTENSILS

Family and friends must be very conscious of the potential danger of sharp instruments that could be used improperly by handicapped people trying to help themselves. Pointed knives, razor blades, needles, and scissors are objects best avoided. When one tries to encourage independent activity on the part of the handicapped individual, there are good and proper subtitutes for these items. If, however, these dangerous items must be used, they should only be used under close supervision and with every possible safety precaution.

BALCONIES, RAILINGS, AND STEPS

In England, there has been a considerable effort to identify and correct serious architectural problems that are potentially dangerous to handicapped people. In many apartment houses, patios and play areas for young children have been constructed with guardrails and concrete designs that are hazardous. In one instance, it was found that the iron guardrails did not offer protection for young preschool children riding their tricycles on the roof play area. Tragically, one child who crashed into the guardrail went through the rail because they permitted the passage of a small body such as his. In other instances, guardrails were found to be too low and children could easily catapult over them in the course of play activities. Some surfaces on roof and balcony areas are slightly sloped, providing an unsteady surface for aged people.

If you are living in a housing unit that provides such areas, don't assume that they are safe. Check these areas yourself and call any hazardous situation to the attention of the authorities. Often, representatives of the health department can be most effective in these situations.

The experience in England has shown that dangerous situations are much more common than any of us realize. They deserve to be analyzed and checked properly.

Windows in high-rise apartments or in any building that has more than one story should be carefully analyzed for safety. In one survey, it was found that high-rise buildings did not provide adequately for the safety of young children playing near the window areas. Children are capable of squeezing their little bodies into very tiny openings, and window areas are often attractive to children. Ideally, windows should be childproof. This means that they should be up high enough to be out of the normal range of children's activities and secure enough so that a child cannot fall out *even if he tries.* Some cities, such as New York, require guardrails on windows that can be opened in apartment buildings where children are living. Check into such an installation if it is not required in your area.

Open stairways should also be carefully analyzed to see that children, particularly handicapped ones, are not exposed to potentially dangerous situations. Stairs that are accessible to disabled people should offer a maximum of protection. Where it is necessary for the handicapped to use stairs, they should be well lighted, offer railings, and provide a good, nonskid surface.

If handicapped children are to be encouraged in normal play, they certainly deserve a safe area for such activities. Suburban families often find that the only place a handicapped child can ride a tricycle is in the driveway. Since driveways normally slope to the street, they often provide a potential hazard to children. Whenever possible, avoid situations such as these and find a more protected area. School yards offer play-area alternatives, since they have a variety of paved surfaces, which are usually in well-protected locations.

OLDER PEOPLE IN AND AROUND THE HOME

In the wintertime, ice becomes a real problem for any handicapped or older person who must use the sidewalk. If the ice cannot be removed, it should certainly be covered with sand or another nonskid material to make it possible for a person to walk on it with safety. Most accidents among handicapped and aged people occur in and around the home. Going to the mailbox for mail in the wintertime, or taking the garbage just a few steps from the house, may provide a hazardous journey for any person if there has been an ice storm or if the area is covered with snow. It is generally better to restrict the movements of handicapped or aged persons under these circumstances.

Basement stairways are generally hazardous, because they are usually open stairways that do not have handrailings or protected banisters. Too many of these stairs are wooden and covered with rubber treads, which often tear and deteriorate, causing a hazardous situation. So far as possible, stairs such as these are best covered with a very tight, close-knit carpeting that provides a firm, yet soft surface. Rubber-backed indoor/outdoor carpeting makes an excellent basement stair covering if it can be tightly stapled or nailed down.

HAZARDS AROUND THE HOME

Throw rugs on slippery floors and any walking surface that is uneven offer potential hazards for *anyone* in the home, particularly the handicapped and the aged. Disabled and older people tend to shuffle and are much more likely to trip when there is a throw rug or an uneven surface underfoot. Avoid these hazards whenever possible.

One delightful older woman of my acquaintance had made braided woolen rugs all of her life. Her home was filled with these treasures, but it was one of the most potentially dangerous places I have ever seen!

Any floor surface that becomes slippery when wet is potentially dangerous. There is much to be said for a very closely woven carpeted surface for handicapped people in the home. Wheelchairs perform very well on such a surface. If the pile is short, handicapped people can generally walk comfortably and easily. A fall on this surface is not nearly so hazardous as on asphalt, tile or terrazzo. Also, these surfaces are much easier to clean and are not easily marked by wheelchairs or shoes.

Seating Handicapped People near Radiators or Fireplaces Is Potentially Dangerous

One of the most vivid scenes in literature is found in Charles

Dickens's *Great Expectations*, when Mrs. Havisham, the suspected patron of Pip, is visited in her old age and gets too near the fireplace. The scene describes in graphic detail the horrors of an old and disabled person catching fire. Such incidents happen entirely too frequently. Ordinary caution in such matters is essential.

By all means, have one or more properly maintained fire extinguishers available in the home. One such extinguisher should be close to the living area of a disabled or elderly person.

Control of Chemicals and Other Dangerous Substances in the Home

When in doubt, lock it up! Medicines, cleaning materials, and any other such substance that may be dangerous should be kept under lock and key if you have any person in the household who might mistakenly use such material. Mentally retarded children often play in areas with cleaning compounds (basements and kitchens) and have been known to swallow toxic materials without anybody being aware of it. Don't let this happen!

People whose eyesight is impaired should not be allowed to take their own medication. The older person stumbling into the bathroom and opening the medicine cabinet in the middle of the night to take his "pills" is a candidate for a serious accident. Medication should be administered by a friend or family member on a regular schedule, with the medication locked up or safely out of the way in the interim. Most pills and oral medication should be administered with ample quantities of water or other fluid. More than one person has choked on a pill he tried to take without water!

Choking

Since many disabled people have associated respiratory and digestive problems, eating simple foods in and of itself can provide some potential hazards. Most people have had experience with someone who seriously chokes at the dinner table.

All family members and friends of disabled people should be familiar with the Heimlich maneuver. This involves wrapping one's arms around a person from behind, making a fist just below the breastbone (sternum), and gently but securely squeezing the person to relieve any obstruction in the digestive track.

Prevention is the best way to avoid choking. Have ample amounts of liquid available during meals, and provide a leisurely and relaxed atmosphere as much as possible. Fishbones and *any* food that has small bones should be avoided when handicapped or elderly people are known to have problems with swallowing.

Know What to Do When These Situations Occur

Rehearse for a choking incident or other accident. Have the phone number of the local hospital or physician readily available in case of emergencies. Keep the car in good running condition and have the gas tank full at all times, in the event you are called upon to get to the hospital quickly.

Special Problems

When a handicapped person or aged person is poor, the usual problems are compounded. Unfortunately, it is true that poverty seems to follow close on the heels of persons with handicaps and many elderly people.

I remember a woman who was quite handicapped by serious arthritis and confined to a wheelchair. I had occasion to visit her home and found her living in a small house with antiquated plumbing. Her usual procedure for taking a hot bath was to heat water on the cooking range and then carry it on her lap in her wheelchair and empty it into the bathtub. When I saw her going through this process with her arthritic hands, I almost died! She was a first-class candidate for a serious scalding accident. Fortunately, we were able to move in quickly and get the hot-water system repaired so that she could avoid this daily hazard.

Another woman of my acquaintance has multiple sclerosis and is confined to a wheelchair in her own home. She has always enjoyed smoking and feels that it is one of the few pleasures left to her. Unfortunately, her hands are very unsteady and smoking is a hazardous activity for her. Her husband allows her to smoke using a cigarette holder and insists that she only smoke in his presence.

The Bathroom

Handrails in the bathroom are probably the most common device to assist aged and handicapped people. They offer a secure handhold that allows one to raise and lower oneself with some security. Give serious thought to how these railings may be used best. Railings can be affixed to the bathtub itself or directly on the walls. When they are being installed, they must be installed with appropriate hardware. More than one family has screwed handrails into wallboard only to find the rail coming loose when it was first used. In most instances, mollies or other more rigid hardware must be used.

A nonskid surface on the bottom of the bathtub is absolutely essential for handicapped people. Bathtub accidents are very common with people who have limited mobility. Don't allow them to happen! You may want to consider purchasing or constructing a simple canvas sling that fits in the bathtub and provides greater security for the disabled person who takes a tub bath. Grab-bars in the tub area are essential.

Where a person in a wheelchair is unable to stand up and see himself in a bathroom mirror, he may be helped by having the mirror tilted so that he can see himself as he washes and shaves.

Low, open cabinet shelves in the bathroom are best for a person in a wheelchair. Medicine cabinets above the sink are almost impossible to use. They often become an "attractive nuisance," since a disabled person may stretch to reach them, endangering himself in the process.

Signal Lights

Nursing homes and similar institutions provide emergency pull-strings in the bath area so that a handicapped or elderly person can signal if he is in trouble. Such installations can be handled by an ordinary electrician and are worth considering.

HAZARDS OUTSIDE THE HOME

If you have occasion to take a person out in the wheelchair, it is often a good idea to either equip the wheelchair with a simple safety belt that fits around the waist, or tie the disabled person into the wheelchair with some inconspicuous webbing or similar material. This avoids the possibility of hitting a rough spot and inadvertently pitching the person out of the chair. Similarly, in any type of vehicle a handicapped person should be securely fixed to the seat. Don't ever consider taking an aged or disabled person into a car without using the seat belts! The aged and/or disabled are prime candidates for serious injury if you have to stop suddenly.

CHAPTER EIGHT

Physical Fitness for the Handicapped

Organic vigor, through physical exercise, is needed to bring an individual up to the highest health level, whether he is disabled or not.

—The author

Does the title of this chapter surprise you? It should not. People who are handicapped have the same need for physical fitness as the non-handicapped. The disabled person's needs are even greater, since circumstances and environment tend to make that person more inactive. This need not be the case.

PRINCIPLES OF FITNESS

The fundamental basis of physical fitness relates to the laws of use and disuse. In simple terms, physical rehabilitation is largely a matter of using anatomical and physiological principles to change a human being for the better. We use these principles every day in our work and play: we use the *overload* principle to strengthen muscles and condition the cardio-vascular system; we use *body mechanics* principles to move and position our bodies most efficiently and with the least stress. In short, whether we know it or not, we use anatomical and physiological principles regularly.

The fact common to all such principles is that the human body is at its best when it is used in a balanced and vigorous way. Atrophy through disuse contributes to tissue breakdown and poor physical health for any human being. Therefore, the need to use the body and keep *toned up* is an essential part of acquiring and maintaining good health. Too often, however, this aspect of positive healthful living is overlooked when it comes to the handicapped or disabled person.

Fitness means the ability of the body to function in an efficient manner without undue stress or strain. It is acquired by bringing *gradual* increases and demands on the body. The consequent building of the cardio-vascular system, muscle groups, respiratory capacity, and other vital systems is what we mean by physical fitness.

TYPES OF FITNESS

Muscle Contour and Tone

The muscles attached to the bones in our body provide the strength and agility we need to perform various tasks. Muscle fitness simply means that the muscles are toned up or efficient enough to do the jobs they are called upon to do. The person who has to lift a heavy object with a certain group of muscles—the flexors in his arms, for instance—needs to train these muscles to lift the amount of weight required. If the weight demand is fifty pounds, it would be appropriate to practice lifting progressively heavier weight with the arm flexor-muscle groups until one has reached the limit of fifty pounds. The way to practice is by lifting weight through the movement several times and then allowing some period for the muscle groups to rest and rebuild. Almost always, this will bring a slight soreness to the muscle groups that are being exercised. Progressively, additional weight should be added until fifty pounds can be lifted comfortably and efficiently.

The overload principle is the method by which we increase our muscle strength and size and bring contour to the musculature of our bodies. People who practice weight training do this in a systematic way to provide handsome physical contours to the body.

A handicapped person is capable of this type of training with whatever parts of his body are able to function. As an illustration, many paraplegics take great pride in the strength of their arms, shoulders, and torso, even though their legs are totally atrophied and will not support them. Many practice progressive weight training.

Paraplegics may also perform gymnastics (such as on the side horse or rings), where less weight in the legs is an advantage. An outstanding performer on the side horse during my youth was an international champion whose legs were atrophied from polio.

Since there is a natural tendency to be less active when one has a disabling condition, progressive exercises can restore strength and contour to almost any muscle group by selective training. The principles used in most weight-training and body-building programs fully apply to handicapped people. Many disabled people keep dumbbells or pulley weights in their homes in order to maintain strength in appropriate muscle groups. Not only is this good for physical fitness, but it adds to their appearance.

A well-built man with a full chest sitting in a wheelchair can be a very attractive human being. If he has developed the muscles in his arms, shoulders, and chest, he looks like someone who has strength. That same individual in an overweight condition would be much less attractive.

Progressive weight training, resistance exercises, appropriate calisthenics, and sports activities that call for muscle skills can greatly aid men and women to achieve a much more attractive appearance and at the same time greatly enhance physical and mental health

Cardio-vascular Fitness

Any prolonged rhythmic activity that brings huffing and puffing is generally good for the heart and circulation. This type of activity is *absolutely essential for the disabled person!* Problems of respiratory-system breakdown and vascular difficulties are often due to inactivity. When a person exercises his internal systems sufficiently to find himself breathing hard and becoming winded, he has probably done enough to have a positive effect on the heart and the related blood-vessel system.

Sustained, rhythmic activity such as walking, jogging, swimming, wheelchair "walking," and similar activities will bring about a good cardio-vascular effect. The movement should last for at least ten or fifteen minutes, and one should experience a good, solid "windedness" before he quits.

Fitness for Sports and Work

Another kind of fitness involves the training of muscles and their coordination to do a specific job. A pole-vaulter will go into training to develop specific muscle groups that must perform well if he is to be a good pole-vaulter. For this reason, he may do a lot of chinning or weight lifting to increase strength in his arms and shoulders. At the same time, he may be building a strong set of abdominal muscles through sit-ups. These muscle groups are all called upon to offer strong bursts of energy in the pole-vaulting event.

Activity and sport fitness simply means training both the cardio-vascular system *and* musculature to perform under prescribed conditions. The person who wants to be an expert swimmer will develop the muscles he needs for a particular swimming activity and the cardio-vascular fitness to go the distance. The best training for any specific activity is the activity itself, taken progressively under training conditions. Adding more weight and speeding up the activity are examples of progressive training.

REGULAR TRAINING

Handicapped people should be encouraged to exercise regularly in a systematic way. This may involve a simple calisthenic routine in the morning and the evening or a much more vigorous program. Bar-bells, pulley weights, stall bars, and chinning bars can be added easily to the home environment. A carpeted floor provides as good a gymnasium as any. Push-ups, resistance exercises, and stretch training can all take place on such a surface.

Wherever possible, handicapped people should be encouraged to indulge in at least one half-hour of vigorous muscle toning each day. All the primary muscle groups of the body should be exercised, including those of the abdomen, which tend to become flabby in a sedentary person.

At the very least, each handicapped person should have all of his joints taken through a full range of movement a dozen or more times each day. Where the person himself may not have the strength to do this, someone assisting him can do it for him. Older people particularly seem to enjoy exercise activities of a mild and moderate nature. Rolling the head around while keeping the neck muscles in tight tension can help to tone these muscles. Doing the same movement loosely can stretch and give a fuller range of motion to the head and neck. These same principles apply to virtually every joint and movable part of the body.

When such activity is carried on in warm water, it becomes especially relaxing. For this reason, swimming pools, jacuzzis, and hot tubs are being used increasingly by handicapped people for relaxation during mild and moderate exercise. If the water is kept on the cool side, additional circulatory benefits are realized. Brisk rubbing after a cool swim or bath serves to tone up the skin and the circulation.

Many handicapped people are now participating in commercial "health clubs." Those who can afford this will find that it provides a needed social outlet as well as good physical training.

Memberships in YMCAs, athletic clubs, and teams are much to be desired. Anything that will get a disabled person moving in appropriate physical activity should be cultivated and encouraged.

OBESITY

Unfortunately, many handicapped people become obese largely because they find eating to be one of the enjoyable activities of life. (Don't we all!) Without a proper balance of big muscle activity, in no time at all a person can become obese. This often adds a *second* handicap to the *primary* handicap.

Diet control for the handicapped is absolutely essential! Disabled people who are obese should be encouraged to lose weight in one of the many programs that are medically recommended. (Weight Watchers has been especially helpful to handicapped women.) Not only is such dietary control essential for weight management, it tends to make one much more conscious of his caloric intake and the content of healthful foods.

Parents of handicapped children should be especially mindful of the tendency for the disabled to become overweight. Mothers of handicapped children who encourage them to clean their plates are not doing them a favor! Children should be taught to eat selectively and lightly when many normal physical activities are not available to them.

If another handicapped member of the family is dieting or on a weight-control program, this can be especially helpful. Having someone to diet with is always easier than dieting alone. Under any circumstances, do all that you can to encourage the handicapped person to remain as physically fit and as weight-conscious as possible.

ACTING AS TRAINER

A friend or family member can often provide the needed encouragement to bring a disabled person into a regular progam of physical fitness. I have seen this happen among young college students who befriended handicapped young people and acted as their trainers.

In one instance, a young man who had been sedentary most of his life found that his trainer, a college student studying physical education, was a real taskmaster. He appeared three times a week and took his wheelchair-bound trainee through his paces: ten minutes of warm-up calisthenics, a quarter-mile wheelchair "run" around an outdoor track, and some body-contact wrestling on the gym mat. Never having participated in these activities before, the young man soon found a new sense of well-being and a buoyant level of physical health that greatly changed his attitude toward himself. This newly found health was evident in his improved physical appearance. The story has a happy ending; he met a young lady and married. Today he is a successful businessman with a family, and, yes, he regularly keeps up his physical-fitness program.

Women should not rule themselves out of physical-fitness programs, especially if they are interested in weight loss and good grooming. Many young handicapped women tend to become careless about their personal appearance. When appearance is enhanced by good health and better fitness, many things improve. The posture of a person is almost always better when his or her muscles have greater tone. We are all "turned off" by the slouching and obese person sitting in a wheelchair. By the same token, we are quite attracted to the vibrantly healthy person who radiates energy.

Often the difference between succeeding and failing in a fitness program is having someone who cares, someone who will help you get started. Any volunteer or family member can become a trainer to a handicapped individual by going through an exercise regime with him on a regular basis. This makes it fun and helps it to become an attractive part of the daily routine.

By providing physical-contact activities, a very useful physical and psychological benefit can often be added to a program. Physical-contact exercises such as dancing, wrestling, joint calisthenics, and duo gymnastics generally help a disabled prson build a better self-image. These exercises should be included in an exercise program whenever possible.

A concerned individual may help a disabled person get into a good fitness program and further encourage him by keeping charts of his progress. You may find it possible to motivate an individual simply by offering to repeat a pleasant physical activity. A long walk in the park can be followed up with a remark like, "Wasn't that great! Why don't we do this every afternoon?"

GETTING OUT-OF-DOORS

Inactive and indoors—this probably describes the vast number of handicapped people, yet there simply is no reason for chronically handicapped people to spend their lives indoors.

Friends and family members make the difference in whether a disabled person enjoys out-of-door activities. Using good judgment, we should make every effort to bring a properly dressed handicapped person into the sunshine. Incidentally, you don't need the sunshine. Many handicapped children have never been out in the rain! How sad it is to consider that there are children who have never known the experience of rain splashing on their faces. Sensitive family and friends will not deny them this experience.

Members of a rehabilitation staff at a special school for handicapped children tell of having planned a summer picnic. When the picnic was suddenly interrupted by a severe rainstorm, all the staff members were discouraged, *but the children had a ball!* Everyone was soaked. They had to scurry for cover, laughing, pushing, running, and falling; it was a wonderful experience that the children talked about for weeks!

Handicapped children and adults alike may especially enjoy weather that may seem unpleasant for most of us. I know one wheelchair-bound young woman who never fails to go out when there is a snowfall.

Winter time is not the forbidden season for the disabled! A warmly dressed handicapped person who has no respiratory difficulties may enjoy cold weather as much as any of us. Unfortunately, too often we are totally unimaginative when it comes to providing ways for disabled people to enjoy winter activities.

I remember ice-skating on our community pond on Sunday afternoon. A wheelchair-bound young man, well known in the community, was there with his family, strapped down in a sled and with a skating "pusher." This young man was having a wonderful time.

Feature articles in newspapers often highlight the activities of legless skiers (advantage: their feet don't get cold!) and wheelchair-bound ice fisherman. Winter activities are only limited by the imagination of friends and family members who must encourage and assist handicapped members to participate.

Here are several good guidelines for outdoor activities:

1. Whenever possible, the disabled person should be encouraged to be physically active when out-of-doors.

2. *Extremes* of heat and cold should most certainly be avoided. Generally speaking, the disabled person who does not have respiratory problems can get along well if properly dressed in cold weather.

3. While encouraging as much independence as possible, be conscious of sensitive areas of health and safety. The disabled person should never be left unattended at the beach or swimming area.

4. If the handicapped person is not able to manage his own clothing, check to see that the person is warm and comfortable in his clothing. This applies to hot weather, too. Most handicapped people do not tolerate extremely hot weather for long periods of time. Keep the head covered in the sun.

5. Plan ahead for personal accommodations when thinking about outdoor activities. If there is a winter outing, a lack of suitable toilet facilities can turn the event into a disaster.

Special outdoors activities, usually announced in the local newspaper, may prove to be excellent recreational opportunities.

Here is a partial list of outdoor activities that can be enjoyed by handicapped children and adults:

shopping-mall circuses;
church carnivals and festivals;
sidewalk art shows;
Easter sunrise services;
Fourth of July exhibitions;
outdoor band concerts;
motorcycle hill cimbs;
fireworks displays;
regattas;
other outdoor sports events, such as football, baseball, and
    soccer games, tennis matches, and golf tournaments;
outdoor museums and arboretum;
zoological gardens;
street fairs;
horse shows; and
parks and recreation areas.

Don't forget picnics—everybody's favorite!

CHAPTER NINE

Helping Handicapped and Nonhandicapped Children in the School

. . . a State shall demonstrate to the Commission that the following conditions are met:

The State has in effect a policy that assures all handicapped children the right to a free appropriate public education.

—Public Law 94–142
The Education for
All Handicapped Children Act
Section 12

Outside of the home, the school is usually the place where a child's attitudes are most influenced and developed. If experiences during the school year are positive, the child is much more apt to enter adult life with good attitudes and positive feelings toward disabled peple. If *practical ways* of assistance are discovered during these formative years, the child is more likely to be a helping and helpful friend to disabled people in his adult life. Wise parents will learn that a so-called normal child who experiences positive exposure to disabled children in his growing years will have a dimension added to his life that will have a salutary influence on *all* of his development. Indeed, many parents seek this experience for their children, and today there is a great interest in doing volunteer work among agencies and organizations serving the handicapped, particularly by youngsters of high-school age.

What is clearly known is that *good attitudes and experiences should begin at the earliest possible age.* To grow up knowing and caring about people who are different is a rich lesson in life. Knowing how to enjoy "different" people is what makes the human experience such an adventure.

BEGINNING IN THE PRESCHOOL

Opportunities for children below the age of five to encounter handicapped and mentally retarded children are rare. Parents, however, can use their ingenuity to provide experiences without having them seem artificial and contrived.

During the 1970s, when day-care and preschool programs were being sponsored under the Headstart program in New York City, a concerted effort was made to have such centers accept handicapped children. It was found that there was great uneasiness about this, especially on the part of the day-care teachers. Early-childhood teachers had not had sufficient training or exposure to handicapped children to be comfortable with them. An experiment was launched where one or two handicapped children were introduced into a group of no more than twenty nonhandicapped preschoolers. Although the program was fraught with problems, many things were learned that are good indicators for parents with young handicapped children who want their children to grow up knowing and appreciating persons with handicaps.

EQUIPMENT AND APPLIANCE BARRIERS

It was found in this experience that the teachers, as well as the preschool children, were frightened of such things as wheelchairs, braces, and the occasional child who appeared in the classroom in a protective helmet, because he was prone to falling and injuring his head. These appliances tended to make the handicapped child appear different. It was soon learned that the best way to make everybody comfortable with this situation was to actually *have them handle and use these appliances.* The nonhandicapped children actually got into the wheelchair and played with it. They helped the disabled child take off his braces, and they became familiar with the protective helmet. Once the mystique of these appliances was removed, there was much more ready acceptance of the children as "normal."

Of course, preschool children have to be taught that special appliances are not toys. The little girl who came in with her hearing aid in a protective harness around her body had problems teaching other children that it was *not* a toy. The teacher helped in this situation, and the appliance was soon treated with the proper respect. A simple and straightforward approach by the classroom teacher was used to teach the children that "Alice needs her hearing aid to listen to the stories."

Before the handicapped children arrived on their first day, the teacher of the preschool program talked about the fact that these children would be different and would need some special help from all the class. She described the condition and showed some pictures of children in wheelchairs and braces. The teacher then discussed some of the kinds of help that would be needed. Immediately, all the children wanted to volunteer to push the wheelchair or help handicapped children in their classroom activities. Once the children arrived and there was some familiarity with the appliances and the special needs, there soon developed a volunteer corps of preschoolers who were good at helping and seemed to enjoy it. No attempt was made to force all children into being "helpers." Some children did it naturally and without any difficulty, while others were much more reticent. In due course, however, a fine atmosphere developed and the classroom proved to be a comfortable and happy place for *all* the children.

PARENTAL PROBLEMS

Unfortunately, in this experience the most difficult problem of acceptance came on the part of the *parents of the nonhandicapped preschool children.* They were not at all sure that having handicapped and/or mentally retarded children in the playgroup would be a good thing. Once again, it related to the problem of fearing the unknown. Since parents in this situation served as volunteers in the classroom once a week, this gave them a direct exposure to the situation. Once involved in the day-to-day classroom work with handicapped children, they became much more accepting.

Parents always want the best for their children, and they quite properly expected that having children who are different in the preschool play group would reduce the experience to something less than they had hoped for. The antidote to the situation often is having an articulate parent of a handicapped child speak to the parents' group. This parent may express *his* feelings about his child coming into a group and being exposed to possible ridicule and misunderstanding.

Once this type of exposure is developed, it is usual that parents of handicapped and nonhandicapped children see and understand that youngsters are children *first*. Certainly, attitudes and acceptance cannot be forced. When there are difficulties in acceptance, it is always best to back off and accept a pattern of *gradual* exposure.

Where the severity of handicap may be so great as to preclude inclusion of children in normal play-school groups, it may be helpful to provide some exposure to such children in other ways. Going on trips together and celebrating holidays, birthday parties and other special events are positive experiences. The nonhandicapped and handicapped children may get to see severely handicapped youngsters who may not be able to communicate or move at all. With proper interpretation and a sympathetic approach by the teacher, this can have a positive effect on young minds. Likewise, severely handicapped children who rarely have contact with normal children of the same age will greatly enjoy and appreciate these contacts.

EXPOSING NONHANDICAPPED CHILDREN
TO HANDICAPPED ADULTS

When I was growing up as a youngster in the city of Chicago, there was a young man with cerebral palsy who sold pencils, shoelaces, and candy from a coaster wagon. He was often seen maneuvering his wagon along neighborhood streets. Although I had great difficulty understanding his speech, I learned to know him as a good person who was trying to make a living. He loved children and would often seek to be in the presence of the young ones. He loved to watch the games and seemed to generally enjoy what bits of conversation we could handle. There is no doubt that this early experience in my life helped to color and influence my own feelings about handicapped people.

Additionally, I was further enriched because I lived just one block away from the Industrial Home for the Blind. Blind people were often seen on the street and in the public park that was directly across the road. As children, we were often asked to help a blind person cross the street or to escort such a person to a store. Although there was very little *direct* contact with the blind in my *preschool* years, the fact was that they were constantly seen as a part of the environment and I accepted them as a part of the world I lived in. I wish every growing child could have this experience.

PRESCHOOLERS PLAY
WITH THE HANDICAPPED

When children below the age of five become comfortable enough to actually *play* with handicapped children, we can be reasonably sure that the nonhandicapped children will not have hang-ups when they grow up. It is when exposure is denied to such children that it becomes more difficult to accept handicapped people as a part of the environment around us. Wise parents and imaginative school personnel will not allow this to happen. They will consider a million and one ways to provide for the rich interchange between the handicapped and nonhandicapped that offers potential for every preschool child in his formative years.

THE SCHOOL YEARS

Since the passage of Public Law 94:142, The Education for All Handicapped Children Act by Congress in 1976, all public school authorities are now required to provide special-education programs for handicapped students who live in their district. This is a matter of law. Ultimately, we will see educational programs for all disabled children in the United States. The form in which such an education is provided may vary from community to community; nevertheless, so-called normal children will undoubtedly have more interaction with handicapped children than ever before.

Handicapped children may be "mainstreamed" in regular school classrooms, or they may be in private or special schools run by the district or nonpublic agencies in the community. What is certain is that virtually all school-age children in the United States will have more exposure to physically handicapped, emotionally disturbed, and mentally retarded youngsters as they grow up.

Making these experiences rich and edifying for both the handicapped and the nonhandicapped youngsters is a great challenge to all of us. "Normalizing" this experience will be the special challenge in the next generation of school-aged children.

HELPING SCHOOL ADMINISTRATORS

Professional educators have been conscious of the problem of handicapped students for many years. There is nothing new about accepting handicapped school-age children into the education milieu. It has been done without any fanfare, and it has been a part of many school programs for years. *What is different now is that it is the law!*

Parents and friends of the handicapped are now called upon to see that the law is enforced, and the reticent school district is encouraged in its efforts to serve the disabled. This support may take many forms. Here are just a few ways you can help:

1. If you are a member of any civic or religious body, encourage that group (Kiwanis Club, Rotary, church organizations, et cetera) to write to the local school superintendent supporting, lauding, and encouraging efforts to serve the handicapped in the district. This type of unsolicited community support is a great encouragement to school boards and school superintendents. When they know that spontaneous support exists in the community for this type of effort, they are much more apt to extend themselves.

2. Invite handicapped children's classes or other special handicapped-sponsored school programs to visit your civic organization.

3. Ask to *visit programs* for handicapped and mentally retarded children in your local school district. If this can be done by organized civic groups or small representative groups from neighborhoods, it is even more effective. Once again, it is *expressed* community interest that adds needed endorsement to these educational programs.

One service club I know invited a high-school class of mentally retarded people to be its special guests for luncheon one day. The speaker was a well-known travel expert. It was an outstanding meeting, meaningful to the young mentally retarded men and women who attended as well as the club members. Needless to say, the school personnel were thrilled with the opportunity.

4. Look for continuing opportunities for association with handicapped schoolchildren. One church group regularly sells the handcrafted wood products made by mentally retarded children at its annual church fair. This gives the church an annual contact with the industrial-arts teacher working with mentally retarded children in the public school. It is a very positive experience that provides a regular exposure to this special-education program.

5. Offer volunteer service to school programs. Special opportunities for volunteer work exist in most public schools. People who have special interests, hobbies, and professions are always in

demand as speakers and "exhibitors" in the schools. When such people specifically request an opportunity to deal with handicapped children, they are usually warmly received.

VOLUNTEER OPPORTUNITIES

Volunteers may also be needed for special school assignments, such as field trips, sports days, and other group programs. One teacher of a high-school class of mentally retarded people has an annual Christmas shopping trip to a large department store in the city of Philadelphia. Experience has taught her that having an adult with each mentally retarded person is essential. Volunteers for this program are always in demand. Those who have participated often say that it is the highlight of their Christmas holiday. Seeing the joy and experiencing the thrill of helping a mentally retarded person buy Christmas gifts for his friends and family is something special.

EDUCATING YOUR
NONHANDICAPPED CHILDREN

Parents with growing school-age children can usually guide the interests of such children in the home. When opportunities for service to the handicapped present themselves, parents can be supportive. Usually the attitudes of parents will influence their children. If, as parents, we find that we are comfortable in our relationships with handicapped people, or at least want to be, then the chances are we will encourage our children to become involved in the problems and rewards that come from working with handicapped people.

Children are quick to pick up anything that might look artificial or contrived. For this reason, it is absolutely essential that children be guided into positive experiences with handicapped youngsters or handicapped adults that are normal and do not look as if they have been set up.

Encourage children to seek out and be a friend to handicapped children at school. A lot of reinforcement may be needed to secure the child's unsteady feelings and his desire to help. Begin by suggesting that your youngster send his handicapped schoolmate a Christmas card. This can be expanded to birthdays and/or special remembrances. A telephone call to such a person might be a good option, especially if the friendship is still budding and there is some lingering strangeness about the person and his condition.

Television programs are often aired concerning the mentally retarded, emotionally disturbed, or physically handicapped. Parents can use these programs as good departure points for further discussion and attitude development.

There are certain assumptions any parent can take for granted in guiding his children:

1. Handicapped and disabled people are almost always lonely and hungry for friendship. Don't feel that you will be imposing yourself on them. It is a rare disabled person who has more friends and social contacts than he can handle.

2. Children need *not* be guided *in detailed* activities with disabled people. Given some general guidelines as to good behavior and conversation, they will find their own (often better) routes of social contact.

3. Most handicapped children and adults would be happy to begin with the existing interests of *your* nonhandicapped child. The preschooler who visits the handicapped older person with his favorite toy or picture book is bringing something very special into the life of that person. He is sharing his interest and enthusiasm.

4. All contacts and relationships should be allowed to develop naturally and not be forced. The child who senses that you are always willing to drive him to see the mentally retarded boy, but are never willing to drive him to his soccer games, will suspect that he is being pushed.

5. Exposure to nonhandicapped growing children is especially meaningful to older and infirm handicapped adults. Almost all older handicapped people live in circumstances that preclude any contact with children. This denies them a vital experience in their

often-bleak lives. There is usually a very natural affinity between older people and young children; however, modern-day living arrangements may destroy this chemistry. Seeing such a relationship develop, flower, and bloom is one of the great thrills of any parent's life.

My English mother befriended two middle-aged blind women when she settled in the United States. These women would come to our home at least once each week for tea. Having grown up in the Jewish ghetto of Chicago, they were thrilled to have tea with a warm and compassionate woman from a different culture. Somehow the "blind girls" always appeared in our home when my brother and I were at home. We discovered that they loved to be around children and that our prattle was very exciting to them. I "warm up" inside when I think back on these experiences.

SPORTING EVENTS

If it is possible for handicapped and disabled people to be transported and moved about out-of-doors, they will love being accompanied to events that young people attend. High-school football games and other athletic events are very appealing. Teenage youngsters may find this a good and natural activity to participate in with disabled people.

A large number of chronically ill people in their middle years are avid sports fans. Many of them follow the major-league football, baseball, and basketball teams religiously. Going to a game with a younger person could be a real thrill. Watching the games on television with a younger sports enthusiast can also offer its own special excitement.

One young handicapped boy who lived on the banks of the Monongahela River in the Allegheny Valley comes to mind. He was an avid baseball fan, and the river barge captains who plied up and down the river with their loads of coal and limestone would talk by two-way radio to Jimmy. The conversation was always about baseball, and Jimmy loved it!

SEEKING OUT THE HANDICAPPED TEENAGER

The adolescent years present a special problem for handicapped or disabled youngsters. It is at this time of self-realization when they must face their own physical or mental limitations. It is also one of the loneliest times of their lives. Whatever effort can be made to seek out handicapped teenagers and draw them into the mainstream of life is a special kindness.

SCHOOLS, CLUBS, AND
OTHER GROUP ACTIVITIES

A wise teacher or club counselor at school can often direct young people into positive involvement with disabled people.

Key Club members who provide a special outing for the mentally retarded provide something very useful for the retarded children as well as the teenage club members themselves. One industrial-arts class in the city of Chicago has a continuing project of building special equipment for handicapped people who are served by a voluntary agency. One Future Nurse chapter in a high school has taken on a special interest in a handicapped person in the community, and members serve as companions for given periods of time. Athletic teams in schools may "adopt" a disabled classmate and take him on athletic trips with some role as timer, trainer, or scorekeeper.

These experiences provide positive reinforcement of attitudes toward the handicapped. Imagination is the only limitation.

CHAPTER TEN

Handicapped People in the Work Place

We are beginning to learn that an "employee" exists only in the realm of job descriptions and organizational charts. It is a person, susceptible to all the pressures of living, who ultimately fulfills or fails at any task.

—The author

Modern rehabilitation services provided to disabled people are generally aimed at bringing them back into the work force. This is a very practical and desirable national policy that is humane, as well as economically sensible.

There is a little doubt that with proper training, appropriate remedial education, and the best of applied modern rehabilitation services, many more chronically ill and disabled people could return to employment. To accomplish this, accommodation in the work place is necessary and receptivity by the employer is essential.

Outstanding examples of handicapped human beings who have taken positions of leadership in the worlds of business, industry, and human services are all around us. This fact does not need to be driven home, except as we see the practical limitations of employment and study the alternatives.

MAJOR OBSTACLES TO EMPLOYMENT
OF THE HANDICAPPED
AND WHAT THE NONHANDICAPPED PERSON
CAN DO

It is true that when unemployment rates are high, we are likely to find a greater number of handicapped people unemployed. Likewise, when unemployment rates are low, there will be more handicapped people in the work force. Just as with the unskilled and poorly educated worker, handicapped people are often the "last to be hired and the first to be fired." Although this is less true than it was a number of years ago, it is nevertheless quite obvious when we examine the reality in employment offices throughout the United States.

In most instances, handicapped people *do* require some special accommodation by the employer in the place of business. Perhaps toilet facilities need to be adapted, special seating must be developed, lighting may have to be intensified, or special accommodations must be made for setting up one's work.

Employers who are in business must make money and are not usually willing to make large expenditures on unproven workers. It is therefore quite necessary that some bridge exist between the *potential for work* and the acceptance of the handicapped worker by a profit-minded employer. This bridge can often be *you*, or a co-worker who is interested in a disabled person.

A sportscaster in a small Illinois radio station prevailed upon the producer of his regular sports show to allow him to air three-minute segments on special sports personalities. After showing a half-dozen three-minute "Sports Personality Briefs" and seeing that the producer was pleased, the sportscaster announced that the man who was making these spots was a paraplegic veteran.

In a pioneering enterprise with the Barnes and Noble bookstores, United Cerebral Palsy of New York City entered into a contract to employ young multi-handicapped people to work in the packaging and shipping department. The agency provided all the supervision and support services, and it was not long before the bookstores recognized the value of these employees and took them on as full-time, permanent staff members.

In each instance, some type of bridge was needed to bring about actual employment. In both instances, *the bridge was either an individual or an organization* that made it easy and practical for the employer to bring handicapped workers into his business.

GOVERNMENT PROGRAMS

A large number of federal, state, and local government programs have been set up to implement special employment programs for handicapped people. The U.S. Department of Labor is the chief resource and key location for the development of such programs. *A handicapped person seeking employment should by all means contact the local Department of Labor office if he is seriously interested in employment or training.* Likewise, employers interested in hiring handicapped people should seek such employees through the Department of Labor by specifying that they would give special consideration to hiring trained handicapped workers.

FAMILY AND FRIENDS CAN BECOME
THE BRIDGE
BETWEEN EMPLOYER AND EMPLOYEE

In many instances, the handicapped person can be greatly aided by the moral and physical support that a friend can offer. Going to the U.S. Employment Office with a friend may make a handicapped person feel more comfortable and secure. Many times, the travel and transportation obstacles are quite formidable and the assistance of an able-bodied person is not only desirable, but essential.

If a person has a handicap which involves a speech impediment, it may be very helpful to have a nonhandicapped friend interpret and speak for him. This may be necessary in the initial and opening phases of contact with the Department of Labor or a prospective employer. Although many disabled people are fiercely independent and resent any help, there are a large number who would welcome it and find assistance of great moral as well as physical value. By offering to help fill out forms, make follow-up calls, obtain civil-service employment lists, advertise for travel and car pools, or assist with similar activities, a person who is used to regular employment can often help the handicapped worker who is entering the world of work. Often the little details cause the biggest problems. These can be avoided by simply having some-one around who cares.

APPROPRIATE TRAINING, ITS USE AND ABUSE

In the highly technological world in which we all live, work training is increasingly important. Handicapped people who are capable of specialized training in *appropriate fields* should be encouraged to take such training. Programs available in the Department of Labor, under the aegis of the Office of Vocational Rehabilitation in most states, are established to provide physical rehabilitation *and* training. Unfortunately, training and addi-tional education are often undertaken by handicapped people in fields that are entirely inappropriate.

The person with athetoid cerebral palsy who cannot hold a pencil in his hand and wants to become a brain surgeon is a classic example of the person with an unrealistic job objective. Yet why should we think this is so strange when this type of individual has probably seen more surgeons than members of any other single occupational group in his lifetime? The matter of vocational guidance is absolutely crucial to the handicapped.

A wise pioneer in vocational guidance, Dr. Shirley Hamlin of Northwestern University, once defined *guidance* as "seeing through John, then seeing John through." This is still pretty good advice.

It is important to understand the handicapped person *first* and then to see that the handicapped person is guided into the right courses in vocational preparation. This is a matter for professionals, yet the well-meaning and properly motivated family member or friend can be influential. Here are some general guidelines that can be helpful in this area:

1. A prospective handicapped worker should have the broadest possible exposure to the field of work in which he expects to be trained. If he is thinking of work in computer technology, he should have an opportunity to see it firsthand and what is involved in a variety of different settings. An hour's visit to IBM is not enough!

2. Training and education fields that are already crowded should be avoided. There are many unemployed handicapped people with Ph.D.'s simply because they are in overcrowded fields. Their lack of employment has nothing to do with their being handicapped.

3. When training may be long and extensive, one should interrupt such training with periods of work in the field to be sure that it is appropriate. Taking a summer off to work in some unknown field is always a wise investment of time and energy. One disabled boy of my acquaintance had invested a year of his life in preparing himself as a journeyman printer. He spent the first summer after his initial training in a small newsprint shop. That experience convinced him that this was *not* the field of work for him, and he changed occupations. It was a wise decision.

4. Where training or apprenticeship is required, it is wise to be involved with a program that leads to employment as a natural course of such training. This is usually a common practice in the trades, less common in academically oriented fields of work. Where training can be combined with an apprenticeship or paid entry into regular work, it is usually highly desirable. It more or less guarantees that the training will end up in a real job.

5. Where employment can be secured in a family-related business or an area where there is a family tradition of work, it is usually a desirable practice. One young man working in the Grumman Aerospace Corporation on Long Island is moderately

handicapped and represents the third generation of his family working in the engineering department of that corporation.

CONSIDERING PART-TIME JOBS

In a very interesting commercial airline trip to one of our southwestern states, I had occasion to speak to the lieutenant governor of one of these developing areas. He told me of a very interesting project he had been discussing in Washington, which involved breaking up many of the full-time jobs in his area into part-time jobs. He saw this as necessary because so many older retired people were now moving into the area and represented a good addition to work force, especially if jobs could be broken up into smaller units.

There is the possibility of many such opportunities for handicapped people. When both employee and employer are not sure of one another, it makes more sense for an employer to enter into a part-time, rather than a full-time work arrangement. Handicapped people would do well to consider this possibility. Although these may not be the full-time opportunities one needs to build financial support and security for life, they often become good entry-level job opportunities, and "getting in" is the big trick with the handicapped.

In some instances, volunteer work may also offer this same possibility. Social-service agencies, religious groups, and artistic and cultural organizations are constantly looking for volunteers. They have been known to employ handicapped people coming from the volunteer ranks once they have proved their ability to do the job.

WHAT CAN I DO AS A CO-WORKER?

Perhaps the biggest obstacle to a full-time employment for handicapped people is the high cost and inconvenience of transportation needed to get to and from the job. Public transportation may be a formidable obstacle to the disabled person. Private transportation, via automobile, is often very costly and may be out of the question if he is working at any entry-level position. Here is where friends and co-workers can be extremely helpful.

Offering to pick up a disabled worker in order to make it possible for him to get to the job may make the difference between his having a job and not having one. A commitment may have to be made for some long period of time to guarantee any security. Nevertheless, it may be something that can be shared among workers on a regular basis. Sometimes simply traveling with another person on public transportation is all that is necessary. Having an able-bodied person there to help is probably the single, biggest assistance a disabled person needs!

Other important assistance may be rendered by offering to help with lunchtime problems, toileting difficulties, or similar obstacles on the job. A thoughtful worker will let the Personnel Office know that he is willing to assist handicapped workers with transportation, feeding, et cetera. This may make the difference between the success or failure of a good employment program. It really doesn't take much! But it *does* take some willingness to be of assistance, and a commitment of time so that the Personnel Office knows you are going to be there for a significant period of time.

BEFRIENDING HANDICAPPED PEOPLE ON THE JOB

After they have successfully found employment, it is unfortunate, but true, that many handicapped people find themselves among the loneliest people in the world! They find that few fellow workers have any social contact with them after hours. Many find excuses to avoid the handicapped during work hours, so their social lives may not be enhanced by having a position in the regular world of work. Here is where real assistance and concern must be developed.

Any person starting out in a new job finds it difficult during the early weeks. Having friendships, associations, and some social contacts is extremely important during these days. For the handicapped, this is doubly true. A compassionate worker who makes an effort to have lunch with a disabled person is really offering him a hand of friendship at a most crucial time in his life.

Don't think that you are being pushy! You can rest assured that your overture will be appreciated. One young woman of my acquaintance who had found a job after many years was brought to tears when her co-workers presented her with a coffee mug with her name on it after the second day of work. She was very touched by this expression of acceptance and kindness. What a simple thing to do!

INFLUENCING THE BOSS

Where your employer has a policy of employing handicapped people, it's a great idea for you to let him know that you think it's wonderful that the company has taken this position. Employers appreciate being told by their employees that they like their policies.

Where a Personnel Office may have gone out of its way to place a handicapped person, you should certainly go out of your way to express some appreciation to that office. At least two labor unions I know of provide special awards to employers who seek out disabled workers. This has done something valuable in building better labor relations between the employer and the union.

If your employer has not made an effort to hire handicapped people, why not call it to his attention in the most diplomatic way? *An industry or business employing 100 people should certainly have from two to six visibly disabled people in its work force.* If these people are not there, you have every reason to call this to the attention of your employer. If you know of an impending vacancy, you may wish to recommend a reliable handicapped worker for the job.

In the long run, this is by far the most effective way to help disabled people find jobs. It is almost always a matter of personal acquaintance and influence. Your influence as a worker should not be underestimated and should certainly be used to bring about the employment of the disabled wherever possible.

CHAPTER ELEVEN

Sex and the Handicapped

Sex ceases to be a devil when it ceases to be a God.
—C. S. Lewis

In the lives of handicapped and disabled people, the subject of sex almost always produces an extreme of either total silence or *so much* discussion that you become sick of it. As in anyone's life, the subject of human sexuality deserves to be understood and integrated into the pattern of life in some balanced and satisfying way. This *cannot* be done outside of a framework of personal standards and the mores of the community in which we live.

Let us assume that a fulfilling, normal, and satisfying sex life includes intercourse with a partner of the opposite sex. It carries with it ideas of responsibility, love, and the old-fashioned word *honor.* Sexual activity relates to the idea of the establishment of family, home, and children and the financial, custodial, and moral commitments these relationships bring.

Although sexual activities exist outside of these standards and human sexuality is learned, understood, and practiced in many different life-styles, for purposes of this discussion we are assuming that the traditional standards of home and family prevail. These are deeply rooted in the Judeo-Christian traditions. *In my judgment, sexual activity is not satisfying to the individual or edifying to society when we live outside of such standards.*

GROWING WITH AN UNDERSTANDING
OF HUMAN SEXUALITY

For very obvious reasons, handicapped children and their families almost always focus on the *disability*, rather than the *ability* of the person. A child in braces going into a doctor's office has an *obvious* physical disability that gets all the attention. I have discovered that many children have secondary health problems that are not attended to because of the preoccupation with the handicapping condition. In a recent survey, one large New York agency serving the handicapped found that a large proportion of the adult women with cerebral palsy had never had a complete gynecological examination. It was obvious that the families of these women saw them as physically handicapped persons with crippled limbs and not as human beings who may have a normal array of ills.

Concentration on the physical disability has often obliterated any thought of sexual problems in disabled people. Indeed, many handicapped children, now adults, testify to the fact that there was almost a total disregard of their human sexuality. They literally grew up as sexual "neuters."

Parents and friends of handicapped children should learn to deal with human sexuality in a normal "growing up" kind of way.

All children play with themselves. They are curious about their sex organs. They are curious about the opposite sex, and it is normal and natural for them to have a lot of questions as they develop. *Learning how to deal with these questions and experiencing sexual development as a natural part of growing up is the best preparation for good sexual adjustment in adult life.*

UNDERSTANDING HUMAN ANATOMY,
ITS STRUCTURE AND FUNCTIONS

However it is represented, handicapped children should grow up with a full understanding of their own sexual organs, how they work, how they look, how they develop, and their potential problems. The best and obvious place for this type of education is in the home, supported by the school. Nevertheless, there is no single place for learning. Children will get a lot of their information from one another. Let no parent doubt that, handicapped or not, his youngster will share information or misinformation with other children. Handicapped children should hear the facts about their own human development from a reliable and accurate source.

I remember the tragedy of a very highly regarded professional worker telling me about the sad experience of a young handicapped woman in her twenties. She had fallen in love with a boy and enjoyed seeing him during the lunch hour at the sheltered workshop where they held hands during their times together. Unfortunately, this young woman had been fed a litany of misinformation and ended each day in tears over the fear of unwanted pregnancy because of this innocent activity. It was a tragic incident.

Sex education has come a long way from an understanding of the male and female anatomy. There are now excellent materials that can be used in the home, school, rehabilitation center, or voluntary agency. Parents have a responsibility to see that children get reliable and accurate information as they grow up. Printed material may be a good way to provide such information.

ATTITUDES TOWARD SEX

It is no accident that most of the jokes in the world are about sex! Sex is funny! Somehow this suggests that perhaps the best attitude toward sex is a more lighthearted approach, neither grim nor giddy.

Sexual activity was and is intended to be the highest of human pleasures; however, *it is not for all people in the world*. There are people who consciously take vows of chastity. They agreed to forego sexual activity for purposes they consider to be higher. This is not to say that all handicapped people should take chastity

91

oaths! It does underscore the fact that a large number of fine human beings in the world are able to cary on meaningful and highly commendable activities without a regular sex partner. *This is a basic fact that all handicapped people should understand.* The unmarried schoolteacher and the celibate priest and nun often have a nobility all their own.

As with eating, there are those who become the gourmets and connoisseurs, those who simply enjoy their regular meals, and those who could not care less about whether they eat or not. Eating can become a grim and tedious process always concerned with calories, cholesterol, and such nonsense, or it can become a pleasurable activity that may be incidental to good fellowship and good coversation. A simple meal might be taken in isolation with simple thanks and private enjoyment. The range of sexual concern and interest is just as wide.

Under any circumstances, an attitude of lightheartedness and conviviality always seems appropriate.

DEVELOPING WHOLESOME ATTITUDES THROUGHOUT ADOLESCENCE

Finding the middle ground of emphasis, neither too much nor too little, and making the subject an easily approachable and lighthearted one may go a long way toward easing the problems that are inherent in adolescence. A young handicapped woman beginning to menstruate obviously needs the assistance and advice of her mother. Failing this, older sisters or other female assistants are necessary to help the woman with the physical job of keeping menstrual cycles hygienic, as well as helping her understanding the process.

Almost all children learn to masturbate and play with themselves at an early age. This should be handled by parents as normal growing-up behavior; however, with more severely handicapped people, this can become a problem.

A young lady recently trained in special education was shocked to find that on the first day of her assignment to a class for mentally retarded children, she was confronted by teenage boys masturbating openly in the back of the classroom. What shocked her even more was the fact that this activity had so little interest for the other students in the classroom. She soon learned that the youngsters had been taught that this was "normal" activity, and *normal,* to the participating children, meant that you could do it anywhere!

Friends and family members must learn to find their own stance with respect to these problems. If we can discuss these issues openly with a teenager or preadolescent, one is always ahead of the game. Many parents have found it useful to rehearse discussions of this kind in front of the mirror. They learn to say the words and watch their own expressions so that they become more comfortable with this type of conversation. This is a good technique!

One mother I spoke to revealed to me that she had always had a problem in using words referring to the sex organs. They embarrassed her and she was never comfortable with these words. It was not until she had rehearsed several "possible" sexual conversations with her son, alone and in front of a mirror, and later with her husband, that she became comfortable with these terms. Obviously, when the opportunity did arise, she was much more at ease with the subject and the use of anatomical language than she would have been otherwise. Some good suggestions are as follows:

1. Use appropriate anatomical language. Avoid the cute childhood phrases that refer to sexual organs. These are neither appropriate nor understandable when one becomes an adolescent.

2. Make sure that the growing handicapped child and adolescent has correct information.

3. Be prepared for questions on the subject of sex. Make sure that your own ease with the subject is apparent.

4. Avoid either too much or too little conversation on the subject. If it is not discussed at all, it probably should be brought up from time to time in some reasonable context. If it is discussed too much, try to dampen the subject as seems appropriate to you.

5. As much as possible, try to make discussions of sex as normal and lighthearted as possible. It should not be treated frivolously, but at the same time it should not be a grim subject. (One parent told me that the discussion of sex in her home had been more funereal than the discussion of death!)

6. It is probably a good idea to have some good information in the form of books and charts in the house. Children should be able to see pictures of their own sex organs and organs of the opposite sex. If these are not provided for in school, they should be available in the home. There is a wide variety of such material now available for children and adolescents. To be effective, the material should be simple, graphic, and *not* medically oriented.

It is good to expose your children to your own attitudes toward sex. These attitudes may not always agree with the textbook. Nevertheless, children should grow up knowing the attitudes of their own parents. If a television program seems to be obsessed with sexual titillation, say so. If you like to read a story where sex becomes a part of the novel, say so. In no instance should your children think that you have superhuman understanding of the subject, control of the subject, or unreal attitudes. Children should also understand where your attitudes come from. If you are a practicing Christian and firmly live in the biblical tenets of sexual relationships, then these should be clearly taught to children as standards you have found to be right for you. If you have rejected these standards, tell them this also.

SEX AND THE UNMARRIED
HANDICAPPED ADULT

A young war veteran of my acquaintance, who is impotent because of his war injuries, once told me that he got at his own problem by realizing that virtually every human being has physical or mental limitations. He was a mechanic of great skill. By his own insightful understanding, he was perfectly clear about the fact that he could never write the great American novel. He related this to his disability and said that he could not be a natural parent of a child, but that certainly did not limit his love for children or his great warmth and understanding of animals.

The truth is that there are compensating factors in life and sexual fulfillment is denied to a very large number of the human race. It may be a potential that we are all born with, but a reality that many are denied. Accepting this and finding satisfying routes of human existence is really the basic job of living successfully. Nobody has it all. Squaring what we do *not* have with what we *do* have is largely the business of living.

Handicapped adults enjoy the company of members of the opposite sex, both handicapped and nonhandicapped. They have the same fantasies that all of us have—perhaps more, because so much of their life is lived in fantasy. They will often appreciate the kiss or the touch more than others. Oftentimes they will read into normal social contacts erotic signals that are not there.

The wise friend of a disabled person will learn to interpret these signs, understand special needs, and treat the handicapped adult in the warmest possible way, while avoiding any misuse relating to sexual overtures. Handicapped men and women can sometimes be taken advantage of by nondisabled people who may feel that they are really doing the handicapped person a favor by participating in some sex act. This is the cheapest kind of rationalization and fits into the same category as taking advantage of an innocent child.

This is not to say that real love relationships cannot exist between a handicapped and nonhandicapped person. They can exist and may be happy arrangements. Unfortunately, they are rare and often fraught with problems. At a time in the world when relationships between people have difficulty surviving under the most favorable circumstances, it seems foolish to invite relationships that pose so many obstacles. Nevertheless, love itself is unpredictable and can overcome the most formidable circumstances.

THE RIGHT TO PRIVACY

Instinctively, we know that sex is a very private matter. The fact that it is private is a part of the special mystery and charm of all sexual acts.

Many handicapped people are denied privacy of any kind. This in and of itself is a very serious problem, since all of life must be balanced between the private and public moments. For this reason, uninterrupted time alone is essential in the life of a disabled person. Where this is not possible because of the nature of the illness, whatever efforts can be made to allow disabled, handicapped, and chronically ill people moments of privacy should be sought.

In many open-ward hospitals and institutions, the problem of privacy is solved by simple screens that are put around the beds. This may be the simplest answer when there is a sharing of quarters or a lack of space to provide needed personal seclusion.

If a disabled person is capable of locking his own door in a private room, he should certainly be afforded this privilege. Parents and friends would do well to assist a handicapped person in finding this privacy if it is not available to him. Be sensitive to this need and handle it in the most mature manner possible; it is an essential element of life.

CHAPTER TWELVE

Transporting and Traveling with Handicapped People

*An efficient and valuable man does what he can, whether the community pays.
him for it or not.*

—Thoreau

The very term "handicapped or disabled" suggests that there is an immediate problem of transportation. Today, coalitions of disabled people testify to the fact that transportation is perhaps the most unyielding obstacle handicapped persons find in trying to enter the mainstream of life. Transportation obstacles present themselves when it comes to obtaining a job, going to school, finding recreational outlets, and obtaining essential rehabilitation and medical services.

Driving along one of our main suburban roads on Long Island in recent years, I stopped to pick up a senior citizen hitchhiker. This was my first experience with an older hitchhiker. He announced to me that he was on his way to the senior citizens center where he had lunch several times a week. His only problem was that he had difficulty getting there. The lack of bus service and transportation often prevented him from obtaining a highly nourishing, low-priced luncheon. He also enjoyed the association with other senior citizens and found that when he could get a ride, it was a "good day."

Transportation problems of this type will continue to persist until such time as mass transit offers accessibility to disabled and aged people. Although federal laws have been passed that prevent discrimination against the handicapped, the fiscal realities at all levels of government have made the development of transportation systems for the handicapped impractical at this point in time. There is some assurance that better days are coming. In the meantime, what can individual friends and family members do to help with this problem?

USING YOUR PRIVATE AUTOMOBILE

When possible, most of us are perfectly willing to use our private automobiles to assist disabled and aged people in getting to necessary services. This is by far the most convenient and comfortable mode of transportation. It is door-to-door service, and, with a sympathetic and friendly driver, it provides some additional special assistance that is always needed by handicapped people.

Many people do not offer this service as quickly as they might simply because they are afraid of "insurance problems." This is a fallacy and should be put to rest whenever possible. A handicapped worker being transported in a private automobile is no more of a risk then any other person. A great many states have enacted "automobile guest" laws that make drivers of private automobiles immune from liability to persons who are riding with them. Indeed, any guest in an automobile has to *prove* "wanton reckless" or "known dangerous condition of the vehicle" to ever consider any liability claim in the event of an accident.

It is reassuring to know that "negligence" must always be proved when a claim of this type is instituted. Although such claims *are* instituted and may be awarded, it is indeed a rare occasion when such an action is brought by a disabled person or his family. Most courts find it very difficult to make an award unless gross negligence is apparent. Remember, this is a condition that exists for *any* guests in your car, not only a disabled person. A handicapped person securely fixed in the automobile by a seat belt, with the driver exercising good judgment, should have no problems.

In many communities, women's clubs and other civic groups have provided volunteer drivers for handicapped people attending clinics, schools, and therapy sessions. Some have done this for many years. In my experience, I do not know of a single legal action that has been brought and successfully executed in these cases. *Volunteer driving is the most convenient and safest transportation that can be offered to the handicapped.*

What *does* become a problem is when a handicapped passenger *is charged a fee for this service.* When this is done, your relationship changes immediately and he is considered to be a paying passenger. This is looked upon very differently by the courts. It is *not* advisable to transport handicapped people in your private automobile for money or other material considerations without thoroughly looking into all the legal responsibilities.

SOME TIPS ON MAKING VOLUNTEER DRIVING A COMFORTABLE AND HAPPY EXPERIENCE

The generosity of people who offer driving services on a regular basis, or even for special occasions, can be enhanced when good preparations are made. Here are some suggestions that can make it a very positive experience for all concerned:

1. Be sure that you have the correct addresses for the pickup and the destination. You should work out the route on a map if possible. The trip can be very disconcerting to a disabled or aged person, most of whom are insecure in strange situations, unless you take a comfortable and easy route. The driver who offers to do the driving and can't find the disabled person's house or his destination can do more harm than good.

2. Allow ample time for the trip, especially if it involves time appointments. If you are driving an elderly person to a doctor's appointment, give yourself extra time to allow for traffic problems and appropriate waiting times. I have seen elderly people delivered

to the doctor's office ten or fifteen minutes late and wondering why their blood pressure was so high! Don't allow this to happen. Give yourself plenty of time.

3. Give special attention to security and comfort in the automobile. Elderly or handicapped people can be very sensitive to excessive heat or cold in an automobile. Be sure they are comfortable, and check on them from time to time.

It is usually a good idea to *avoid smoking* when transporting disabled people. Also, the radio should be kept at very low volume or not used at all during such periods. Be doubly sure that the headrest is up, seatbelts securely fastened, and the sun visor is down if you are driving into bright sunlight.

4. Moderate your speed so that you drive somewhat slower when transporting disabled people. We all tend to drive too fast. With a passenger in the car who may be especially sensitive, it is a good idea to reduce your speed by at least 10 MPH. This may seem uncomfortable to you, but it can be the difference between a pleasant ride and a harrowing one for the handicapped passenger.

5. Under no circumstances offer to drive disabled people in your automobile unless the vehicle is absolutely safe.

6. Try to seat men and women where they are most comfortable. This is one of those silly little things that often make a difference to the person's self-image. Many adult males like to sit in the front seat of an automobile, especially if there is a male driver. Ladies often enjoy being transported in the rear, where they feel somewhat special. Explore these ideas. Ask your passengers where they would prefer to sit.

7. If you are transporting nonhandicapped people along with the disabled, indoctrinate them concerning some of these rules before the ride. An unthinking passenger might be a chain-smoker and unconsciously make the ride very uncomfortable for an elderly person who is not used to being in confined quarters with smokers.

8. Use every precaution when loading and unloading. Make sure that the automobile brakes are fully set, the car is in parking gear, and there is no chance of rolling accidents.

9. It is usually a good idea to take an umbrella along if you expect bad weather.

We must recognize that an automobile ride can be a real threat to an aged or disabled person. Make it special in every way you can. This assistance is a part of the special helpfulness we are all endeavoring to bring into aged and/or disabled people's lives.

PUBLIC TRANSPORTATION/ HAVING SOMEONE ALONG

When it becomes necessary to use public transportation, most handicapped people find it very helpful to have an ablebodied person along to assist. Nothing more than this is needed. Having accessible trains, taxis, and buses may be *less important* than having an able-bodied person at one's side throughout the trip.

If you are assisting, try to develop a system that is comfortable for both you and the handicapped person. If he is immobile or slow, ask him if it is easier for you to hold his arm or if it is better for him to hold you. Most disabled people prefer to hold someone else and resent being pushed or lifted by other people.

If you are assisting a person onto buses, trains, elevators, or any vehicles with automatic doors, stand directly in front of the door so that it will close on *your* back if it does close. Don't allow a handicapped person to be jarred by a rapidly closing automatic door. Even though such doors will not injure people, it can become very disconcerting to a disabled person if he is unable to get out of the way.

This is often the clue. You are, in a sense, "running interference" for the handicapped person throughout his ride. You may have to extend an arm or turn yourself to offer some interference to a crowd, a door, or a running child to prevent the handicapped person from being bumped or frightened. You can do this quite easily and courteously with a little practice.

The trick in traveling with such a handicapped person is to travel as a companion and not as a monitor or "sick person's nurse." Once again, this takes a little practice. It means that one should engage in light and appropriate conversation that is not always concerned with the disabled person's health. (Remember those trips as a child when Mother was always asking how you were?)

As much as possible, note a route before you start the journey. This may mean equipping yourself with street maps, subway maps, bus routes, and other useful information. Telephone calls in advance can avoid problems of canceled trains, buses, et cetera. Remember that aged and handicapped people *are* insecure in strange situations. If *you* are also insecure, it compounds the problem.

It is sometimes very helpful to let some of the parties you will be seeing know the circumstances under which the handicapped person is traveling.

I remember working in a rehabilitation center in Central Illinois. The chief physical therapist was very upset about the fact that one of her female patients was always late for appointments. The therapist complained about this, but since the patient was a very quiet person, the therapist got very little in the way of response. On one occasion, we had an opportunity to go to the patient's house and actually pick her up for her therapy appointment. She found that her patient was living in a fourth-floor walkup apartment and required someone to assist her down four flights of stairs. In addition, there was no waiting vestibule and it was necessary for the woman to stand out-of-doors in all types of weather while she waited for a taxicab to get her to the appointment. Needless to say, the therapist felt very differently about the situation once she understood the circumstances.

Where it is possible, notify a waiting dentist, medical doctor, or other professional person that you will be accompanying the disabled person on the appointment and that you may be coming by a difficult transportation route. It can help to reassure everyone that you intend to make the schedule while notifying them that it may be a difficult journey. *Planning ahead* is really the key to success in assisting disabled people with their transportation problems.

TRANSPORTING ELECTRIC WHEELCHAIRS
AND OTHER MECHANICAL DEVICES

Since electrical wheelchairs are generally energized by wet batteries, any tipping of these batteries may spill acid on floor surfaces and cause serious damage. One must remember this and try to avoid any problems of this kind whenever possible. If the transport of an electric wheelchair is required, the battery should be removed in advance and carried on some secure and level surface, such as in the trunk of a car. Simple battery handles are available to lift the battery out of the chair in these circumstances. The same precaution may be needed with other transportation devices, such as the commonly used "Amigo" and other motorized vehicles. Generally, all of these are designed with transportation capabilities and you should understand them before undertaking their movement.

It is usually a good idea to have *two* people available for lifting these more involved wheelchairs and mechanical devices. They are usually heavier and much less wieldy than the simple folding wheelchair. Pushing an electric wheelchair up a ramp that cannot make it under its own power may also require more than one person. Be prepared for this.

TEACHING HANDICAPPED PEOPLE TO DRIVE

Virtually every state will allow handicapped people to operate a motor vehicle on their own if they can pass an appropriate driver's test. One does not have to be ambulatory to pass these tests. In many states, there are special instruction courses and testing arrangements. As a general rule, handicapped drivers are known to have good records when it comes to automobile safety. They are usually cautious and careful drivers, and once you get past the handicapping condition, you can be assured that a handicapped driver is perfectly safe to ride with.

One sad story occurred in a Michigan town where a boy with cerebral palsy, who had been certified to drive his own automobile, stopped for gas. The attendant had never seen such a disabled person driving an automobile and immediately became concerned. He called the town sheriff who appeared on the scene and promptly arrested the person with cerebral palsy for being intoxicated. Not understanding the condition, the sheriff took this young man to the local prison, where he held him for several hours until he was reassured that the cerebral palsy was a permanent handicapping condition and the young man was capable of driving an automobile.

These are unfortunate circumstances and still occur entirely too often. Handicapped drivers generally carry some special identification on their license or vehicle that indicates that they are qualified to drive an automobile. Where special adaptations, such as hand brakes or steering knobs, are required on the automobiles, these are usually provided. Where handicapped people have little mobility, they often equip their automobiles with Citizen Band (CB) radios or similar equipment so that they may obtain help in emergencies.

In a lifetime of work with handicapped people, I do not know of a single serious accident that was caused by a disabled driver! This must mean something.

ADAPTING SPECIAL VEHICLES FOR
PERMANENT USE

With the advent of the van, popularized in some TV programs, many handicapped people have now discovered that a van can be customized for their special use. At a recent exhibit in England, I noticed that half the exhibit hall was filled with specially adapted vehicles of this kind now being sold in the United Kingdom. These vehicles can be a great boon to handicapped people's traveling. Special seating and elevator lifts make it simple for wheelchair-bound and other types of handicapped people to use the vehicles if they have the use of their hands and are able to drive. Some vans accommodate simple mobile homes and include specially adapted toilet facilities and cooking arrangements. Rehabilitation publications and special magazines serving the handicapped often carry ads for such vehicles. The handicapped person who is able to drive a vehicle and may have constant need for such transportation would be well advised to consider the possibility of owning such a vehicle.

USING PARKING SPACES
FOR THE HANDICAPPED

Throughout the United States, most communities have developed special parking spaces for handicapped drivers. Usually these are authorized under special local ordinances. Wherever possible, one should inquire into the local regulations that govern the use of such spaces. A person who regularly drives a disabled person to shopping centers, places of worship, or recreational facilities should qualify for the use of these spaces. Such facilities are intended to be a convenience to disabled people without any regard for who may be providing the transportation! If you are a regular driver for a handicapped person, by all means see to it that you are qualified to use these facilities. They were designed for your convenience.

CHAPTER THIRTEEN

Accommodating Church Life to the Handicapped

The Person

Speak to me not of withered limbs
And eyes that cannot see.
These say nothing of who I am
Or what I yet can be.

Speak to me not of my slow tongue
My smiling face—a mask.
These tell none of all my dreams
Or how I do a task.

The cover on the book is not
What carries on the tale.
It's only in its pages
That the mind can set its sail.

My body's just a cover
And it's all that you can see.
But it's in my heart and spirit
That you'll find what's really me.

—The author

It is no accident that the many stories in the bible about handicapped people and their encounters with prophets, disciples, and Jesus himself, indicate that these handicapped people were out of the mainstream of community life—outside the city, outside the temple, indeed, seemingly outside of God's love.

How do we create changes that can bring disabled people into the mainstream of congregational life today?

There is growing evidence that congregations all over the country have begun to address themselves to the problem—and the opportunity! The international symbol of access, the graphic wheelchair, is now appearing on bulletin boards and other congregational property. This wonderfully healthy sign signals a renewed interest in meeting the spiritual needs of special people.

Unfortunately, too often a congregation will perceive its ministry with the handicapped as a simple architectural problem, when it is a *series* of problems—in architecture, attitude, communication, and transportation, to name a few. How can the average church or synagogue deal with them?

GETTING ORGANIZED

Most congregations have one or more members who have a special interest in the problem because of having a handicapped child or an aged parent, or being involved with some special-interest group related to disabled people. These are the people who can get things started. They can become the nucleus of whatever committees may be needed. *The important initial thing to concentrate on is getting handicapped persons to the congregation.*

CONGREGATIONAL SURVEYS

Responsible trustees of any congregation will ask the question, "Just how many people are we talking about?" or "How do we justify expenditures to change church architecture when we are unsure of whether there will be handicapped worshipers after we have made the changes?"

Conducting a survey of congregational members and friends and their special needs *may* be a helpful first step. But: we suggest caution in putting too much credence in such surveys, since it is likely that (a) handicapped people are not members of the congregation because they have never been able to get in the door and (b) there is a danger of considering the problem not worthy of attention unless there are significant numbers needing help. (If only one person needs help, it is worthwhile!) Also, what of future needs?

Probably the most significant effect of a congregational opinion survey is that it creates an awareness of the problem. Simply by raising questions concerning disability one begins to arouse a concern. A sample survey used in a Long Island church may be found at the end of this chapter. When it was taken, this survey indicated that there were relatively few known handicapped people in the congregation. The group most in need of some special consideration turned out to be the older members!

ARCHITECTURAL PROBLEMS FIRST

Initial activities will probably be a consideration of architectural problems. Religious buidings have formidable architectural obstacles: numerous stairs, poor toilet facilities, narrow aisles with short seats, and virtually no provision for meaningful worship by persons who are blind or deaf or wish to sit in the congregation with a fidgety mentally retarded child. This creates some de facto obstacles that are undoubtedly the main reasons why handicapped people and their families are usually not seen in corporate worship.

TO RAMP OR NOT TO RAMP

The symbolic wheelchair can often become tyrannical in our thinking! A congregation with one or two members in wheelchairs can often be trapped into a simplistic approach to the problem. This may reduce action into building a ramp so that these wheelchair people can get into the sanctuary. Think twice before you use this approach!

Ramps may be perfectly acceptable in many cases. They may also destroy the aesthetic value of the buildings, create a hazardous surface in icy weather, and require someone with herculean strength to move the wheelchair into the building.

There are additional approaches. Simple low-rise lifts or elevators may be much more sensible. These do not create hazardous surfaces when it is icy and they can be installed either indoors or outdoors. They provide for one or more persons being securely lifted up to about six feet. One prerevolutionary Presbyterian church in New York State found this to offer a much more acceptable access than a ramp.

Ramps require a grade of no more than 1 to 12 and should have handrails and offer a good nonskid surface to be effective. Several grades should be broken up with a "landing" so that there is not a long and formidable course.

SEATING AND ACCOMMODATION IN THE CONGREGATION

Assuming that it is possible for a disabled person and/or his family to enter a place of worship, is there suitable seating in the sanctuary itself? Could a person with crutches or canes or a person in a wheelchair find a suitable seating area without a great deal of fuss? Often the answer to this probem is relatively simple. It involves removing part of a fixed pew row in favor of comfortable movable chairs.

Where does the mother who would like to attend worship service with her young mentally retarded child sit? Can she find a place where she would not be embarrassed by the child who inadvertantly cries out during the service?

One church I know has built a simple glass partition at the side of the sanctuary where mothers with babies and young children may sit without any fear of disturbing the service. It is no accident that young couples with infants are always in attendance: they are provided for!

Where there are known needs, these can be met individually with a little imagination. The person who is totally deaf may be a good lipreader and simply needs to have a clear view of the speaker's face unobstructed by microphones and lectern lights. Important parts of the worship services should be typed out and pew rack bibles (in large print for the visually impaired) be provided.

Blind people often appreciate hymns in Braille, or in large print for that large group of legally blind. Providing such aids says "Welcome!" to the blind worshiper. The Southern Baptist church publishes the entire hymnal in a dozen Braille volumes. Every worshipping congregation should have at least some such aids. A member expert at writing Braille may volunteer to create such aids for a weekly service.

TRANSPORTATION PROBLEMS

How do handicapped people get to a place of worship? If there are no family members who regularly attend, it is difficult. *Usually this is the biggest single obstacle to participation in church life.* It requires a regular *system* and *commitment* to some type of transportation outreach.

The problem may be addressed in several ways:

1. Individual members may take responsibility for transporting disabled people to functions in their private cars. There are no insurance problems in doing this.

2. This activity may be a special responsibility of some such organization as the deacons, women's association, or other group.

3. If the number is great, a special vehicle may be leased for this purpose. School buses and ambulettes that regularly transport handicapped people in wheelchairs are often available on weekends! Lease arrangements may be possible at low rates.

4. Regular taxi service may be provided to disabled people, with the church paying the bill.

Any of these approaches must be organized and carefully monitored to see that it is doing the job. Costs and reliability are the two chief issues.

ATTITUDINAL PROBLEMS

Let's face it, whether members of a religious body or not, most people are simply not naturally comfortable in the presence of handicapped individuals. People require an orientation-and-accommodation program if they are to welcome and accept handicapped people. Here are some suggestions:

1. If there are institutions in the area, such as homes for the mentally retarded, schools for the blind or deaf, or people with cerebral palsy, the congregation may extend a special invitation for the handicapped to participate in worship on an "Access Sunday" or some other special event. The handicapped and their families should be invited to the service and hosted at some social function following the formal worship.

Don't start with the worst problem first! Ten drooling and grimacing severely mentally retarded and physically handicapped clients can be a real "turn-off" to a congregation as a first introduction. A group of deaf children with a sign-language interpreter may be a better *initial* approach. Use judgment when you begin such activities.

One church I know invited a group of young mentally retarded adults living in a new community group home to participate in its worship service. The retarded guests were well dressed, under good supervision, and seemed to enjoy the fuss that was being made over them at the coffee hour that followed. This had a highly salutary effect on the congregation and did much to break down initial prejudice toward the group home being there in the first place.

2. Have a disabled minister or lay member speak from the pulpit. A person with an obvious disability who speaks knowledgeably may be a wonderful help in developing proper attitudes. Such people are living "success stories" and have great meaning to a congregation. Unless the person is unusually skilled or highly motivated, a simple statement of appreciation at being a part of a worshipping company is a sufficient subject.

3. Films on the subject can be built into regular church programs. As an illustration, a women's association may study the special needs of the handicapped in the community for a year or more. As beneficial as this may be, we must remember that nothing is quite the same as having real-life personal contact with disabled people. Problems are solved only when we face them in the flesh.

4. A wheelchair obstacle course on church property may be a "fun way" to get into the issue. This technique has been carried out very successfully by voluntary agencies interested in having groups understand the problems of wheelchair people.

The process is simple: A wheelchair "obstacle course" is laid out in the building or on the proprty so that nonhandicapped members will have a chance to get into a wheelchair and go through a course, which may take them five minutes. This will give them some feel for what it is like to be in a wheelchair and the problems posed by even the simplest tasks, such as turning, going up a slight incline, getting through a door, having a drink of water, et cetera. Youth groups may find this an especially good activity to sponsor. It provides for more understanding of the handicapped.

Nothing is more self-defeating than approaching this subject in a grim fashion. Anything that can be done to lighten the issue is usually to the good.

Similar "simulation games" can be devised for other types of disabling conditions. A simple map that explains how a wheel-chair person may get into and about the building is useful. Inserted in the bulletin from time to time, it becomes a reminder that there is a program for handicapped people who need special accommodations.

Reminders of special transportation needs of the handicapped, or opportunities for services to the handicapped (a blind member might need a regular "reader"), are also good bulletin inserts from time to time. The big trick is to keep a congregation *conscious* of its opportunities to serve disabled people.

SUMMARY

Any group of people who are serious about accommodating the needs of persons with handicaps must recognize that it is a long-term commitment. Some programs may be tried and fail. Try again! Even by trying we offer a sincere hand of fellowship to the many disabled who long to be part of a worshipping congregation.

"ACCESS" QUESTIONNAIRE

___ Chronic physical
    disability
___ Mental retardation
___ Mental illness
___ Learning problems

___ Social dislocation
___ Problems of aging
___ Sensory problems (vis-
    ion, hearing, or speech)

Have these problems prevented participation in church life
(here or elsewhere)?

    ___ Yes   ___ No

Rank the following needs according to priority (1—most
urgent, 2—next in urgency, etc.).

___ Wheelchair accessibility to the sanctuary and facilities.
___ Suitable transportation for aged and infirm persons
    attending worship and other functions.
___ Tape-recording ministry of worship services and church or
    Sabbath school for shut-ins, permanent or temporary.
___ Outreach to physically and mentally handicapped *not* now
    in our congregation.
___ Special seats and seating access in the sanctuary for
    disabled people.
___ Designated parking areas for disabled worshipers.
___ Church programs to better understand "Barriers to
    Access" in the church.
___ Special church school classes for the disabled where
    indicated.
(a) ___ On our own   (b) ___ In cooperation with
                                       other community
                                       churches

Sample Congregational Survey:

____ An active ADVOCACY program to promote the rights of the handicapped in our country.

Other problems or needs _____

_____

I am willing to work on the "Access" project (specify interest areas).

_____

Name (optional)

CHAPTER FOURTEEN

Technical Aids: The New Frontier

A mute and paralyzed 13-year-old cerebral palsied boy will "speak" and "chant" Sunday at his Bar Mitzvah in Pittsburgh, using a specially adapted computer that generates an electronic voice.

—USA Today
October 24, 1985

A growing array of electronic devices and mechanical aids have the potential for revolutionizing the lives of disabled people. New lightweight metals and plastics have replaced the heavy braces we once saw on handicapped children, motorized vehicles that look like scaled-down golf carts now travel the streets with their paraplegic drivers, and people with communication problems carry small communicators the size of pocket calculators to aid them in producing understandable speech. As exciting as these developments are, they are only signs of even better things to come.

Because we are at the cutting edge of the revolution in rehabilitation engineering, it is necessary to better understand some of these technical aids and how to handle them. It will become *increasingly* more important as technological developments provide better bridges between handicapped people and their environment. The simple fact is that there are many handicaps that cannot be changed in any way, *but the environment in which the handicapped person lives can be changed!* Changing the environment is what technical aids are all about.

116

SIMPLE DEVICES

"What are those two long sticks with the hoops at the end? They seem to have some cloth material wrapped around the hoops. Are they something you use in your everyday life?" These questions I posed to a young handicapped woman more than twenty-five years ago. The sticks and the hoops were a simple device she and her family had developed to assist her in putting on silk stockings without the aid of another person. A family member simply rolled the silk stockings around the hoop at the end of a day. Each morning, Barbara was able to put her foot into the hoop and, pulling the stick up, release the silk stockings. Her job required that she be dressed formally, and without this device it would have been difficult for her to find someone to assist so early in the morning.

Consider Alfred, who required a hot bath every evening because of his physical problems. Alfred was sixteen years of age and did not appreciate having a family member assist him with his bath. An unusual aluminum contraption in the bathtub with a canvas sling was a "bath aid" that provided a secure place for Alfred to sit and bathe himself each evening. It was made by an electrician friend who had seen the problem and developed a simple solution to meet it. The "bath aid" gave Alfred the independence and the privacy he required.

These are samples of simple, nonmechanical devices that may make a great difference in the life of a disabled person. There are literally thousands of such devices. Unfortunately, there is not a central place where one can purchase or find out about such equipment. This problem is being addressed seriously in a variety of public and private quarters and undoubtedly will be met more effectively in the years to come. However, at this writing, there is no central place where one can find out about *all* such equipment.

Organizations serving the handicapped, clubs and groups made up of handicapped people, and some recent publications, may catalogue this type of material. Some of it costs pennies and can be developed at home quite readily. Others require more specialized tools and are more difficult to manage. Here is a sample of some of the simple devices I have seen effectively used by handicapped individuals:

1. elastic shoelaces that make it possible for a disabled person to put his feet in tie shoes without bending down to fasten them;
2. hand-operated extension clamps that can be operated from a wheelchair to pick up objects from the floor or off shelves;
3. Japanese-style socks that separate the large toe from the rest of the toes and allow a person without hands to use his feet to grasp objects;
4. a rubber ball fitted to the handle of a spoon or eating utensil, making handling the spoon much easier for the person who has extreme muscular weakness or spastic movements;
5. dishes and plates with suction bottoms that allow them to be fixed to the table so that they will not move if tipped or pushed too hard by the disabled person;
6. a rubber-tipped head stick that allows a person to use his head to type, turn pages, or point when he does not have the use of his hands;
7. a special glove designed to hold a pencil and crayon when a hand is not strong enough to do it alone;
8. covered nonspill cups and glasses that allow sipping and drinking without fear of spilling;
9. long and flexible drinking straws that eliminate the need for lifting a cup or glass during a meal; and
10. swiveled eating utensils that are balanced so that there is no danger of tipping food from the spoon or the fork.

One mother I know used unbleached muslin to make a simple harness for her adult daughter so that she could turn in bed at night without fear of falling. Since the girl was spastic and had uncontrolled movements, this simple device offered a measure of security for the girl and her mother that allowed them both to get a good night's sleep.

These are but a few of the many simple day-to-day pieces of equipment that have been found to help handicapped people. Some of the most effective devices have been invented by friends and family members who have simply addressed a problem faced by a handicapped person by adapting common materials to meet the need.

When day-to-day problems of care and management are clearly defined by family members, it is remarkable how often solutions can be found to these problems by inviting the participation of friends or other members of the family.

MECHANICAL AND ADAPTED EQUIPMENT

From the use of simple household items, to more sophisticated equipment, one can develop a "bioengineering mentality." *If we cannot change the handicapped individual, we can change his environment.* This can be done by mechanical, electric, electronic, and even chemical technology. There are many examples of technical aids that help the handicapped apply these principles.

Typewriters can be fitted with guards so that uncontrolled movements of the fingers do not eliminate the efficiency of this kind of communication. Typewriters can be fitted with many devices, including some that will require a key to be held down a certain length of time before it actually types. Expanding the typewriter keyboard, or miniaturizing it, are both examples of what can be done to existing mechancial devices to make them respond to the needs of a handicapped user.

Popular among today's technical aids are a whole array of environmental controls. These are electric, mechanical, sensory processes used to turn on lights, raise the blinds, signal for help, control the television, or otherwise more effectively use the existing systems available in most households.

A growing number of kitchen- and bath-installation specialists are now familiar with the special requirements of the handicapped homemaker. Countertops that permit a wheelchair to roll *under* the counter are now available. Special knobs to keep senile people or mentally retarded children from turning on the oven or cooking range are also on the market.

Although it is not our objective to fully describe the vast array of mechanical and technical aids available commercially, it may be helpful to simply list the areas of care into which utilitarian devices fall:

1. aids for feeding;
2. aids for toileting;
3. aids for bathing;
4. environmental controls;
5. communication devices; and
6. mobility devices, including electric wheelchairs.

The telephone company now has a wide variety of special equipment for handicapped phone users. If you have not been in touch with your local telephone company recently to assist in this matter, it is a good idea to contact them. Technological improvements have been remarkable over the past few years.

Since many devices to assist the handicapped are made outside the United States, there are often problems of appropriate electric circuitry, special variations required by electrical and plumbing codes, replacement parts with metric measurements, and the general problems of language that occur in translating technical manuals. Examine these problems before investing in foreign-made devices.

DEVELOPING ACCEPTANCE
OF TECHNICAL AIDS

One cannot assume that simply because a technical aid is available to a handicapped person and is appropriate to him, it will necessarily be accepted and used. Disabled people may absolutely turn their backs on any technical aids, preferring to struggle along whatever way they can. However, when independence is a goal, a handicapped person will usually seek out technical aids and bioengineering equipment to assist him in his day-to-day activities. Oftentimes the attitude of a friend or family member is crucial in helping to develop proper attitudes.

Any person must learn not to be afraid of mechanical or electrical equipment. The first time there is the slightest malfunction, many people tend to discard what may provide very useful assistance. All mechanical and electronic equipment require some getting used to, some training, and some proficiency in order to make it an effective part of one's life.

A New York city rehabilitation agency installed more than twenty Swiss self-cleaning toilets in its rehabilitation facilities. In planning for the facility, it was thought that these devices would offer a measure of dignity to handicapped people who required another adult to clean them after a bowel movement. Since this device would eliminate this necessity, it was assumed that it would be well accepted. After the initial year, the agency discovered that the self-cleaning toilets were seldom used. It was found that an orientation and training program was necessary for the staff before *they* could be comfortable with this new device. When such an orientation period was completed, the staff felt much more comfortable in using these devices with their handicapped charges.

ELECTRONIC EQUIPMENT

Electronic technology has exploded in the United States in recent years, and a new generation of electronic devices has emerged for the benefit of disabled and handicapped people. The application of this new technology is still in its infancy; however, there is very little doubt about the fact that it holds great promise for the future.

Joel sits in his chair in front of a special word processor. Before him is a device that looks like a typewriter fixed to a television screen. On one side is a simple tape-recording device. With the interfacing of these devices, Joel is able to type at a fairly rapid rate, simply by using a suck-and-puff mouth switch. As the light travels over the board, Joel "puffs or sucks" to register a character, a word, or a symbol on the screen. When he has composed an appropriate letter, picture, or design, he simply puffs his signal and prints the message. Should he wish to keep this communication in the "memory," he puffs the appropriate signal and this is accomplished.

The type of device I have just described is presently being used by a number of handicapped people in this country and abroad. It is one of a new generation of such devices. With the slightest control of a single body movement (a blinking eyelash will do), control of such equipment can be realized.

SPIN-OFFS FROM THE SPACE PROGRAM

The technology developed in the United States space program has created many possibilities for handicapped people. Unfortunately, many of these are not yet cost-effective. This poses one of the large unsolved problems we face, since there is very little possibility that such equipment can be mass-produced and thereby reduced in cost. In spite of this, the technology is "on the shelf" and stands a good chance of being used in a variety of special programs in the future.

Much attention has been paid by the news media to special scanning devices that make it possible for a blind person to read from the printed page. Now a similar device has been developed for the speech-impaired. A simple reproductive sound mechanism is able to translate printed words into a voicelike sound.

By special computer receiver, a wheelchair is controlled by voice commands. The command can be programmed to any language or form of oral communications. Such is the electronic technology that presently exists in experimental form.

WHAT CAN A FRIEND OR FAMILY MEMBER DO TO HELP A HANDICAPPED PERSON "PLUG IN" TO TECHNOLOGY?

Develop a system enabling you to become as knowledgeable as possible about such equipment. This may start out with a simple shoe box or desk drawer to receive the clippings of magazines and newspapers advertising specialized equipment. Taking out a subscription to a rehabilitation magazine that carries ads for specialized equipment is another good way to keep current.

Where possible, visit manufacturers' showrooms or exhibit areas where you may have a hands-on experience with mechanical and electronic equipment. Although you may not be a rehabilitation expert, you will soon learn whether a given piece of equipment or a technical aid will have application to the disabled person you know.

WHERE TO LOOK FOR HELP

In every community there are people who are anxious and willing to help develop, adapt, or repair technical aids that can serve the handicapped. Such groups as the Telephone Pioneers of America (retired telephone-company employees) have active programs in the development of equipment to serve disabled people. A Pennsylvania chapter of the Telephone Pioneers built a large clocklike device with a turning pointer and a number-alphabet code. By controlling this pointer, a young boy with cerebral palsy was able to develop a reasonably rapid communication system. It was a vast improvement over the old "word board" that he had used in a lap tray on his wheelchair.

Many times a high-school industrial-arts class will undertake to assist with a special project within its capabilities. Specialized seat inserts, wooden wheelchair trays, and car seats for handicapped children are examples of such projects I have seen developed in school shops.

INTERNATIONAL RESOURCES

A number of countries in the world have approached this problem more effectively than we have in the United States. In some Western European countries, there exist data banks for the cataloguing of equipment resources. A surprising number of technical aids are available in the Western European countries. Sending information requests to the health and social ministries can often produce helpful material. Through such an inquiry, a young paraplegic man discovered a Swiss electric wheelchair vehicle that suited his purposes beautifully.

In many developing countries where technology is not advanced, one can find examples of very simple and effective approaches to technical aids. Since the vast majority of these countries are agricultural rather than industrial, their approach to technical aids is more oriented to an agrarian society.

Combining the agricultural technology from underdeveloped countries and the gardening technology in places like the United Kingdom, one can often put together the aids and technology to make possible such things as simple outdoor gardening pursuits. I remember seeing a young boy with cerebral palsy in Macedonia, Greece, caring for rabbits on his father's farm. This boy would have been totally out of place in anything other than a rural setting. Simple adaptations made it possible for him to work effectively as a part of his father's farm-labor force.

Vacations abroad often provide an opportunity to see the approaches used by different countries and cultures to the problems of the handicapped. A friend or family member who brings back information from a foreign land to assist the handicapped enriches that person's environment in a very real way.

MAKING IT WORK

Friends and family members who have an interest in handicapped people should stay alert to the fact that there are many therapeutic devices that simply do not work for *all* disabled people. Recommendations from physicians or other medical personnel do not always insure against inappropriate devices.

Wherever possible, commercially available equipment should be tried by the disabled person himself before it is purchased. Where this may not be possible, the equipment should be seen by someone who can make an appraisal of it. It is an unfortunate fact that many handicapped people have closets full of unused equipment that was inappropriately purchased because of the great emotional attraction of such equipment. The sensitive and wise family member and friend of the handicapped will avoid these problems.

CHAPTER FIFTEEN

Advocacy: A New Word, an Old Idea

Definition: Advocate—one who takes up the cause of another.
—Webster's New Abridged Dictionary

People have been taking up the causes of handicapped persons for as many years as history itself. The Bible is rich with stories of advocates—those who spoke or acted on behalf of the blind, the mentally ill, or the physically handicapped. This role is both the easiest and the most difficult for those who care about disabled people. We quite naturally speak and act on behalf of persons who cannot speak for themselves. Nevertheless, being an effective advocate requires more than good intentions and oftentimes is a course filled with hazards. Well-intentioned advocacy can very easily backfire and cause more problems than it solves.

The city of New York is a case in point. In recent years, advocates of wheelchair-bound, physically handicapped persons became quite vocal about the need for curb cuts at major street corners. This would obviously make it easy for people in wheelchairs to get up and down curbs and assist mothers using baby carriages. The city responded to this request and began a program of providing curb cuts at major corners. Unfortunately, they did not consider the blind person who found that tapping his way to a corner now became difficult because there was no curb! One disabled group was helped to the disadvantage of another.

ORGANIZATIONS AS ADVOCATES

Probably one of the most effective ways to assist the handicapped is to join groups and organizations given to this task. The actions of many are often better than individual actions. A number of organizations now represent disabled people. These are nationally recognized charitable organizations that have been in existence for many years. Others are more recent coalitions of disabled people themselves who "advocate" a specific course of action related to their own welfare. More informal local organizations have also developed throughout the country in recent years.

Identifying with an organization interested in the affairs of the handicapped can be a most rewarding experience. There are those who attest to the fact that this activity has given new meaning to their own lives, benefiting them as much as it has the handicapped. An obvious advantage in joining with others is that your advocacy is not solely dependent on your own activities. Most organizations welcome volunteers. If you have had experience in government or have been involved with such things as consumer protection or legal aid, you have some valuable experience to bring to an organization.

Most of the positive achievements on behalf of the handicapped have been brought about by organizations that have developed their resources specifically to focus on some large unmet problems. In Pennsylvania, parents of mentally retarded children took their youngsters to meet legislators on the weekends. This activity was primarily responsible for bringing about special-education legislation in this state. Another voluntary group interested in the handicapped was instrumental in developing state-by-state legislation to require immunization against rubella (German measles) in young female students.

Many of the new laws affecting civil rights of the handicapped were introduced because of coalitions of disabled people working throughout the United States. These coalitions are active in most of the countries in the western world. They have made their mark on the national laws that affect their lives.

SMALL AND INFORMAL GROUPS
AS ADVOCATES

Improvements in community life for the handicapped population need not relate to the large national organizations. Many community groups have been formed to bring about important local changes. Several townships on Long Island, New York, now employ staff members to deal with the special problems of handicapped people. This was brought about through a growing awareness of the special needs of disabled people, articulated by the activities of community groups.

Newspapers often carry the story of an injured high-school athlete who suffers a permanent disability. His friends form a club to raise money for his care and provide help on a personal basis. Such groups are among the most influential advocates, since they have such a clear focus for their activities. Achieving this clarity of focus and determining what is right to do present the most difficult problems in advocacy.

Consider an example from the Defense Department: no Pentagon general would ever advocate a wholesale purchase of army tanks without first taking a prototype tank into the field for extensive testing. Yet in services to disabled people and in social-welfare causes generally, this is almost never done. One of the strongest and most defensible advocacy positions that can be brought to legislative and judicial bodies is the insistence upon prototype and pilot programs that test ideas *retail* before they are implemented *wholesale*. Groups advocating for the welfare of the disabled have a responsibility to *make sure* that what they are asking for will work and truly serve the best interests of disabled people.

In one unfortunate experience, a coalition of handicapped groups insisted that a major city install elevators at all of its subway stations. This was done at great cost to the city. It was everyone's expectation that this would produce a viable transportation alternative to people in wheelchairs and other disabled people. After almost ten years of experience, it has now been found that each elevator is used so seldom as to suggest the closing of the elevator service. More in-depth research would have shown that the real transportation problem was in getting *to* the subway stop!

Whether in small and relatively informal local groups or in large national organizations, it is imperative that well-meaning people interested in bettering the lives of handicapped persons be sure of their ground. *We must know that there is value in the programs being advocated.* The best way we can know this is by testing such programs in demonstration projects.

In becoming an advocate for a handicapped person or a handicapped group, we usually find ourselves directing our efforts toward improving or changing laws and government regulations. This can be done by direct concentration on the legislative leaders or direct contact with administrative leaders in government (such as mayors, governors, and even the president of the United States), or it can be done by bringing legal action through the judicial system. Some wisdom is necessary to know which approach has the most chance of success. It is obvious that some political savvy and good judgment are required.

In recent years, a greater number of legal actions have been directed toward improving the lot of handicapped people. Federal, state, and local laws prohibiting discrimination against disabled people are now being tested in the courts. Advocates for disabled people may find themselves treading their way through the judicial system when they become involved in this process.

INDIVIDUALS AS ADVOCATES

Two handicapped people had been denied service in a downtown restaurant. The manager of the restaurant had simply decided that having disabled people eating in his establishment would be disconcerting to other restaurant patrons. Friends of this couple were told about this situation and went to the restaurant manager. He changed his attitude quickly when he saw that his

129

discriminatory action had a ripple effect on many people.

A well-dressed and articulate young woman accompanied her disabled friend when she attended city-government hearings concerning Medicaid payments. This friend's presence made a vast difference. She was able to speak for the handicapped woman, and there was an implied threat that if the situation was not satisfactorily resolved, there would be continuing efforts to change it.

These are good examples of how single individuals can effectively take up the cause of a disabled friend.

We should not assume that all advocacy is aimed at governmental forces that portray our government as the villain. Well-meaning charitable organizations themselves may need some reminders from time to time. It is astonishing to me how many cultural, religious, and educational institutions need to be reminded of a handicapped person's needs and rights.

A student calling on the president of a university to remind him that blind students cannot use the elevator in one of the buildings because it has no Braille-code pushbuttons is a good advocate. The parishioner in the local congregation who writes to the trustees to tell them about a church entrance that is inaccessible to nonambulatory worshipers also becomes an advocate.

Children themselves can become very effective in this role. A nationally known youth-serving agency arbitrarily decided that a young handicapped boy could not participate in its program. The children themselves brought action against this national organization to include this handicapped young man in the program.

In most instances, a friendly (but determined) approach to the hierarchy of any organization is sufficient. If a response is not forthcoming in a reasonable time period, additional action may be necessary.

Public officials have just as much concern for disabled people as the rest of us do. However, by virtue of their responsibility, they may need specific direction and fiscal guidance when it comes to change. It is quite obvious that the larger the dollar investment required, the more we are apt to find resistance. When one advocates for a reasonable course, even though it may involve large expenditures, constant and reasoned pressure is most effective. This is not to eliminate the ultimate threats of demonstrations and legal action. These may be called for at times; however, most officials will respond to reasonable requests by reasonable people.

GOVERNMENT AS AN ADVOCATE

There is now a large body of law that undergirds each disabled person and his family in the United States. Government is responsible for seeing that these laws are implemented. Laws against discrimination or deprivation of service must be enforced. An advocate for a handicapped person may play his most important role by simply calling to the attention of public officials cases where the law is not being kept. In a blatant case of discrimination, the advocate should call this to the attention of an appropriate regulatory authority.

It is surprising to see how voluminous are the laws of local, state, and federal-level governments that protect and provide for disabled people. It is generally a good idea to arm oneself with copies or summaries of such laws to begin with. They can be obtained by writing to local, state, and federal offices. Legislative representatives may also be contacted for this type of information.

People with special skills can often be effective in serving as advocates and friends of the disabled. A practicing lawyer may very well be the best person to take up the cause of a handicapped individual who has legal problems. A family member speaking to his state legislative representative about his problems is most effective in his role as a constituent. A doctor pointing out inadequacies in medical service, an architect indicating inaccessible public buildings, and the businessman speaking to his associates about discriminatory hiring practices affecting the handicapped are all examples of special people doing special advocacy jobs.

An internationally known minister in one of the leading church organizations in the United States was born without arms. He has become a most effective advocate for disabled people throughout the world. His approaches are mainly directed to church-related groups where he has the greatest influence. He jokingly says, "They trust me because they know I have nothing up my sleeve."

Elected officials who themselves have handicaps or have a handicapped child in the family have been among some of the most influential leaders in the public sector. The fact that Franklin D. Roosevelt was confined to a wheelchair had great significance on the times in which he lived and his effectiveness as President of the United States. Although his disability was veiled in his public appearances and news reports, subsbseqent generations have come to realize the severity of this man's handicap. He couldn't stand without assistance and was totally dependent on others for his mobility.

WHEN LEGAL ACTION IS NECESSARY

Deciding to bring any issue to the courts means making a serious and long-term commitment. Litigation is usually quite costly. Persons considering this course should recognize that it is a last resort. Legal actions brought by organizations are generally superior to those brought by individuals, since litigation can be protracted and involve enormous amounts of time, money, and people. Although successful litigation may create precedents that have far-reaching effects on future generations, one must count the costs before embarking on this course.

Legal Aid Societies and similar legal-assistance groups, such as the Civil Liberties Union, may be helpful when one is considering litigation.

A handicapped person may not have *special rights* under the law, yet he can always defend his rights under the constitution. This is the general and broad premise on which most litigation rests.

Do extensive homework before you consider a legal redress of grievances. There are some broad premises that have been reasonably well established in law and on which the rights of handicapped people may rest:

1. the right of every child to a free education at public expense in the most appropriate manner;
2. the right of a handicapped individual to live in the community in the least restrictive environment;
3. the "right to know," allowing parents to have access to a handicapped person's records.

REHABILITATION INTERNATIONAL CHARTER FOR THE 80s

Rehabilitation International is a nongovernmental, worldwide organization whose members include a majority of United Nations member countries. One of the most clearly stated documents relating to the problem of disability, and necessary steps to meet it, is contained in the declaration of Rehabilitation International in its Charter for the 80s:

DECLARATION

More than five hundred million people are disabled in the world today. In every country at least one person in ten is disabled by physical, mental or sensory impairment. They share the rights of all humanity to grow and learn, to work and create, to love and be loved, but they live in societies that have not yet learned to fully protect those rights for their citizens with disabilities. They are too often denied the opportunities and responsibilities which should be theirs.

More than three hundred and fifty million people with disabilities live without the help they need to enjoy a full life. They live in every nation, in every part of the world, but by far the greatest number live in areas at early stages of economic and social development. Here poverty joins with impairment to poison the hopes and diminish the lives of children, of adults and of families.

An estimated twenty-five percent of the members of any

133

community are prevented by the existence of disability from the full expression of their capacities. This includes not only people who are disabled, but also their families and others who assist and support them. Any society which fails to respond effectively to these problems accepts not only a huge loss of human resources but a cruel waste of human potential.

Throughout history, humanity has erected barriers both physical and social which exclude from full participation in its communities those judged to be different because of physical or mental variation. Buildings and transportation are mostly inaccessible to many people with disabilities. Information and beauty do not reach those whose sight or hearing or comprehension is impaired. The warmth of human association is withheld from children and adults whose physical or mental capacities are different from those of the majority. Education, productive employment, public service, recreation and other human activities are denied to many or permitted only in segregation. For people with the most severe disabilities, who are unlikely ever to be capable of independent activity, there is often total neglect or insufficient effort to assist their personal development and improve the quality of their lives.

The knowledge and skills now exist to enable each country to remove the barriers which exclude people with disabilities from the life of its communities. It is possible for every nation to open all of its institutions and systems to all of its people. What is too often lacking is the political will to proclaim and translate into action the policies necessary to bring this about. A nation failing to respond to this challenge fails to realize its true worth.

Poverty and war not only cause disability but also affect the availability of resources for its prevention and rehabilitation. The aims of this Charter require for their fulfillment, therefore, a more equitable distribution of the world's resources and relations between nations that is based on reason and cooperation.

In this new decade it must be the goal of all nations to reduce the incidence of disability and to evolve societies which will respect the rights of persons with disabilities and welcome their full participation. For these purposes, this Charter for the 1980s is promulgated. It aims, each of equal importance and priority, can be achieved only when there is a basic modification of each society's attitude toward disability and of its response to the problems of handicapped people.

The aims are:

- To launch in each nation a program to prevent as many impairments as possible and to ensure that the necessary preventive services reach every family and every person.
- To make certain that every person with a disability, and every family which includes a member with a disability, receives whatever rehabilitation service and other support and assistance may be needed to reduce the handicapping effects of disability and to make possible for each person a full and a constructive role in society.
- To take all necessary steps to ensure the fullest possible integration of and equal participation by people with disabilities in all aspects of the life and a constructive role in society.
- To disseminate information about people with disabilities and their potential, and about disability, its prevention and treatment, so as to increase public knowledge and awareness of these problems and of their importance to every society.

Each country is urged to prepare a comprehensive national plan for the achievement of these aims in the light of the principles enunciated in this Charter and of its own circumstances. The plan should involve all major sectors of national life and be a component of high priority in any programs for national development; it should provide for the full participation of people with disabilities in such programs.

It is essential that each country should have within its government an office or an individual of senior rank, directly responsible to the Head of State of Government, as is appropriate, to direct the preparation of the national plan and to coordinate its implementation this office or person should be assisted by a national advisory body including representatives of all relevant government departments, organizations of people with disabilities, and voluntary and professional groups.

The Charter for the 80s is a statement of consensus about measures to enable humanity to protect and nourish the rights and responsibilities of every person, those who are called disabled and those who are not.

CHAPTER SIXTEEN

Handling Finances

He who would be wise, let him learn to handle money prudently.
—Benjamin Franklin

Because of the enormous responsibility of dealing with a handicapped condition itself, families who have a handicapped member often neglect other important aspects of his life. This is true when it comes to the management of money.

Handicapped children are often denied the usual opportunities of learning how to manage money in their growing years and may come to adulthood with little or no experience. It is very important that handicapped children who are capable of learning about finances be given regular opportunities to make decisions about money during their growing years. Too many disabled adults are forced to handle their own financial affairs with virtually no experience. Many social agencies have instituted programs to teach elements of financial management, including such simple things as handling normal checking and savings accounts.

Families and friends of handicapped children can serve as useful teachers by creating opportunities for the stewardship of money. If such experiences are regular and systematic, they go a long way toward preparing the disabled person for the financial realities of life.

One friend of mine who is in the printing business helped a young handicapped teenager develop his own greeting-card business. By providing quantities of greeting cards and setting up a mail-order and telephone business, he gave a young home-bound person valuable business experience that is certain to help him in later life. The amounts of money are really not very important during the growing years; the management experience is what is essential.

LEARNING ABOUT MONEY IN THE HOME

When disabled children live with their own families, many of the usual things done with children can be modified in regular home-life patterns. Providing children with a weekly allowance always serves as a good teaching device for young children, handicapped or not. Having a given amount of money on a regular basis provides basic experience in management. When discussions are held in the home concerning buying, selling, spending, and costs, such family conversations offer good opportunities for financial instruction. Allowing a handicapped child to make his own decisions about purchases affecting his life, such as clothing, schoolbooks, and even medicines and therapeutic devices, can also be very helpful. If a child is capable and mature enough, he may be given responsibilities affecting fiscal affairs of the family as well.

With the advent of mail-order selling, handicapped people now have expanded opportunities to select merchandise and make appropriate purchases.

In many suburban communities that do not have a central downtown shopping area, comparative shopping for some goods and services may be essential. This can often be done most readily over the phone or through mail-order catalogues. Here is a place where a handicapped person can really shine.

An enterprising handicapped college student in the Midwest recently set up a shop-at-home service business. He does comparative shopping for his friends and neighbors who need auto and home supplies and/or personal services. He receives a percentage of the "savings" realized on their behalf.

Opportunities for part-time work for children who have disabilities are very limited. Nevertheless, an imaginative group of friends or family can be of real assistance in this area. Most children have some experience with magazine subscriptions, greeting cards, Christmas wrappings, or cookie sales. They sell the merchandise, collect the money, keep a percentage, and submit the balance to the supplier. Disabled children can participate in these activities just as well as, and often better than, children without handicaps. The telephone and the mail become their chief vehicles for selling. Family and friends should be helpful in these enterprises and suggest and encourage them where appropriate.

Be sure that children's sales opportunities are legitimate and the profits from the activity are meaningful. Adult decisions may be required to prevent handicapped people, particularly children, from being exploited.

LONG-RANGE PLANNING BY FAMILIES OF THE HANDICAPPED

No question is asked more often then, "What will happen to our handicapped child after we are gone?" This is the largest burden that families of the handicapped face. The uncertainties of the future, and particularly the financial uncertainties, weigh most heavily on families with disabled members. What can they do?

Although this section is not intended to be a fiscal-planning document best developed through professional accountants and lawyers, some conventional wisdom may be helpful.

When there are brothers and sisters in the family, they can usually play a role in guiding the financial destinies of disabled family members. However, many families have attested to the fact that brothers and sisters often become unreliable when they get older and have their own families. Also, many parents would prefer to relieve their other children of this responsibility and turn to professional money managers, organizations, or charitable institutions to do the job.

Under most of the social programs serving the handicapped in the United States today, a person with financial assets must first use these assets before he can become eligible for any public programs. In many ways, this becomes a penalty for thrift and prudence in providing for a disabled person. It is not unusual to find a provident middle-class family who have squirreled away resources to provide for a handicapped child only to discover that the child is *not* eligible for many of the public programs because he has financial resources of his own. Families are learning that financial resources left to a disabled person become liabilities rather than assets!

At this point in time, most families with disabled children would do well to leave their assets to persons and institutions *other than the handicapped individual* in order to qualify for the considerable resources available in the public sector. These public resources should be thoroughly understood before any long-range family planning is done. Public programs are available for subsistence, housing, work training, medical services, and a host of specialized programs designed to enrich and expand life for handicapped people.

Friends and family members of the disabled can be enormously helpful in discovering eligibility requirements for the various public programs. They can also research the options for conserving financial resources by speaking to bankers, lawyers, and other people in appropriate occupations. This is a complex matter and should be researched as early in life as possible.

Since laws and programs change, a financial program should be reviewed periodically so that the disabled person is left with the most current plan upon the death of his parents. It is an unfortunate reality that many well-meaning parents have had their plans tied up in litigation for years while a disabled child struggled to meet his own needs. Although professional help should be sought in most of these matters, members of a person's immediate family, other relatives, and friends have a much more personal interest in the matter and usually do best in setting up programs. They generally have an intimate knowledge of the people concerned.

There are many fiscal devices an individual or family may use in establishing trusts or similar legal arrangements to manage money on behalf of a disabled person. Any plan requires continuous and prudent management. The big trick is setting up the most appropriate management that will have the best interest of a disabled person at heart throughout his life. Many national charitable organizations have now set up departments to deal with this problem. Banks customarily have trusts departments, although these tend to become somewhat impersonal and costly.

FINANCIAL AFFAIRS OF
HANDICAPPED ADULTS

When a handicapped person has neither the judgment nor the mental faculties to manage his own financial affairs, it is important to have a reliable person or organization in charge of his resources. In most instances, this is a charitable organization or private institution. However, it can also be a friend or relative.

Many people today have had the experience of aged parents who become senile and require someone to manage their financial affairs. Families often stumble through this process, and many find themselves with unexpected taxes and bills at the end of the person's life. These are pitfalls that can be avoided with some prudent planning.

As early as possible, some responsible family member should be designated to act as the custodian of an individual's resources *when there is reason to expect management problems.* A mentally alert handicapped person going for a period of prolonged surgery, an aged parent entering senility, a disturbed adult entering a mental hospital—these are all examples of situations requiring others to take over the management of financial affairs. When such a choice can be anticipated or expected, don't delay! It is very important to divert assets into a system that can be managed by others.

Where judgments may be impaired and one wants to conserve the independence of the handicapped individual, simple plans may be made to require two signatures on checks and other documents. Most disabled people, even under deteriorating circumstances, like to have a little cash in their pockets. This should not be denied them. Nevertheless, it should be carefully monitored by some loving and rational friend or family member. It is an unfortunate truth in today's world that handicapped and disabled people are prime targets for the unscrupulous. Many have been victimized, tricked, and robbed by dishonorable people who recognize them as easy prey. By all means, protect against such possibilities.

SOME SPECIAL WAYS TO BE HELPFUL

If you have skills or interest in financial mangement, it is important to offer this skill to the disabled person. Simply asking, "John, would you like me to help with your budgeting?" is always in order. Many times, disabled people generally appreciate this kind of help. Once you are invited into the financial world of the disabled person, you will undoubtedly find many ways to be helpful.

It seems that disabled people are prime candidates for "get rich quick" schemes. I have had my heart broken on many occasions when a disabled person has told me about following up on a magazine advertisement that promised large returns for telephone sales and home envelope addressing. In more instances than not, these programs have ended up *costing* the disabled person money that he could ill afford. Having a friend to discuss and review these situations with would prevent much of this.

If in your own personal experience you have found useful banking services or financial-management procedures, you might suggest these to a disabled person. As an illustration: many banks offer programs that directly receive social security checks, thus avoiding the possibility of mailbox thefts. If you have found this to be helpful, you might suggest it to a disabled person.

Offering an opportunity to shop with a disabled individual is always a nice thing to do. Your judgment in the selection and pricing of merchandise can be very educational to the disabled person. Make your own feelings known, but allow judgments to be made by him.

Provide as much help in the process as possible. Send for mail-order catalogues that he can review. Manufacturers involved in mail-order sales of clothing often send samples of fabrics. There are salespeople who provide home sales for various products.

If the salesperson can be prepared in advance, so that he doesn't expect too much from a disabled person, having the Avon representative call can be very enjoyable.

Above all, make anything having to do with money as enjoyable as possible. Financial matters should not be grim! By making money management as pleasant as possible, you will be encouraging the development of another dimension in a disabled person's life.

CHAPTER SEVENTEEN

Sorting Out Your Feelings

A friend loveth at all times.
—Proverbs 17:17

Understand from the beginning that no person attempting to assist handicapped people will meet joyous and uniform success with every endeavor. It is highly likely that most people who enter into some commitment to be a friend to a disabled person will face frustration and disappointment and end up with mixed feelings. It is true that the so-called "helping professions" attract a disproportionate number of people who enter this type of work because of their personal needs rather than their altruistic motives. This isn't always as negative as it might seem. Many people who attempt to help others because of a need to feel superior or heroic soon find that they themselves are being ministered to by the personalities of disabled people. I have heard testimonials from people in all walks of life admitting that their motives for helping handicapped people were initially quite selfish. Fortunately, many found that ego feeding was not compatible with service to the handicapped. In more instances than not, what started out to be a rather selfish motive turned into a very high purpose.

One need not be too analytical when it comes to examining one's motive. There are many who simply like to work with disabled people and others who just want to be helpful. If your hands are there to help disabled people, consider this enough.

TIME-LIMITED COMMITMENTS

A very highly motivated community leader in a midsized community confided to me at one time that she had enjoyed many years of voluntary service to handicapped people. Her biggest problem was that she now knew it was time to quit and did not quite know how to go about it. Unfortunately, too often in voluntary endeavors, there is never a graceful way to "get out." For this reason, it is important to set some time objectives for your activitites. Committing yourself to a year or two of voluntary work with handicapped people may give you a concentrated experience that can be unusually productive. Most of us like to sense achievement from our voluntary and charitable activities. When one sets a time limit, one is more apt to work for a positive experience and solid achievement.

At least one men's service club I know of makes this problem very manageable by its own membership credo. New members of the service club pledge to provide at least two years of voluntary service, totaling 100 hours a year, as a condition of membership. This pledge carries over a two-year period and is renewed voluntarily at the end of that time. Renewal of the service commitment is *not* a condition of membership after the first go-round. The net effect of this policy is to provide a meaningful service commitment on a *mandatory* basis, which is usually followed by a commitment on a *voluntary* basis.

We must face the fact that not all people will enjoy their contacts with disabled persons. Disabled people can be just as difficult as nondisabled people. Personality conflicts may arise. There are those who will find that they just cannot be around disabled people for any protracted period of time. Insisting on a continuing association when these conditions exist is foolish. One should recognize, without guilt, that experiences of this kind may fail. There are no guarantees of success, but everyone owes it to himself to try being a friend to a disabled person.

DOING THINGS IN SMALL QUANTITIES

Any initial effort in a personal relationship with a disabled person should provide some time limits which are manageable and can be realized. One well-meaning person I know recognized that a disabled community member needed regular transportation to the train station in order to get to his job. He offered to do this daily driving. Unfortunately, he did not say how long the offer would stand. The handicapped person assumed that it was a permanent commitment and was very chagrined to find that after several weeks of regular transportation, his friend found this inconvenient and simply called one morning to break it off. How much better if he had said that he would commit himself to transporting the handicapped person to the train station for the next two weeks.

If any assigned or self-imposed commitment is made, be sure it is done in a comfortable period of time where the commitment can be fully met under the most pleasant circumstances. Nothing is less appreciated than an unreliable volunteer! Be sure you are a *reliable* volunteer for three weeks, three months, or a year, rather than an *unreliable* volunteer over a ten-year period.

HOW LONG SHALL YOU CONTINUE?

So long as the experience provides some meaningful assistance to a disabled person and can generally be handled comfortably by you, there is good reason to continue. If a disabled person becomes demanding in his attitude or if the service commitment becomes burdensome, it is highly likely that the relationship between you will break down. You should quit before this happens.

One of the cardinal rules in voluntary work is: "If you can't meet the commitment, find your own replacement." This applies to relationships with disabled people. If you are regularly providing a driving service or other voluntary work on a regular schedule, by all means back up your activities with others who can be there when you are not. If your interest is real and enthusiastic, it is likely that you will be able to find others who will enjoy sharing responsibilities with you. However, if you are "fed up" or discouraged, finding someone to carry on may be difficult.

It is generally a good idea to think about how you will get *out* of an activity when you are thinking about getting *into it*. It defines the commitment at the very outset. Here are a few questions you might ask yourself from time to time to see if you are enjoying the experience:

1. Do I look forward to my voluntary commitment and anticipate it with some happiness in my weekly schedule?
2. Do I talk about the experience among my friends on social occasions?
3. Do I really feel that my involvement with handicapped people is helping them?
4. Can I point to some important lessons I have learned that make me a better person through this experience?
5. Are there additional experiences that I would like to "go on to" in this same area?
6. Has this experience whet my appetite for more information about disabled people?
7. Do I feel that my friends envy me in this activity?

If your answer to most of these questions is "yes," then it is likely that you are finding your experience rewarding and worthwhile.

Recognition is a basic human need and should be accepted as a part of what may come naturally from voluntary service. One need not feel unduly embarrassed because his voluntary work is publicly recognized; however, a secure and balanced individual will not need to be recognized for everything he does. Nevertheless, all of us want a pat on the back once in a while, especially for the good and useful things we do with our time. Learn to accept such recognition gracefully and with style. Many times a handicapped person himself may find that this is the best way he has of expressing his appreciation.

In a recent ceremony conducted by a voluntary agency for one of its outstanding volunteers, the handicapped clients who had been served by this volunteer sat in the front row with tears in their eyes. Those tears expressed far more than the accolades and the plaque.

Most of us will have to forego public recognition when we endeavor to become a good friend to a handicapped person. The only recognition we are likely to receive is the warmth of a personal relationship.

In a rather ordinary incident on a busy day in New York, I had it all come together. I spotted an older handicapped woman descending a short flight of stars in front of a transient hotel. She was in braces and used crutches and was obviously having difficulty coming down each step. Since I was walking by, I stopped and offered to assist her down the last few stairs. She turned with the brightest face and said, "Thank you for offering, but I am all right—and thank you for the smile." It was the first time in my life that anyone had ever thanked me for a smile. Reward enough? You can find it too!